HOW
TO ACT
LIKE A
CEO

OTHER BOOKS BY D. A. BENTON

Lions Don't Need to Roar

How to Think Like a CEO

The $100,000 Club

Secrets of a CEO Coach

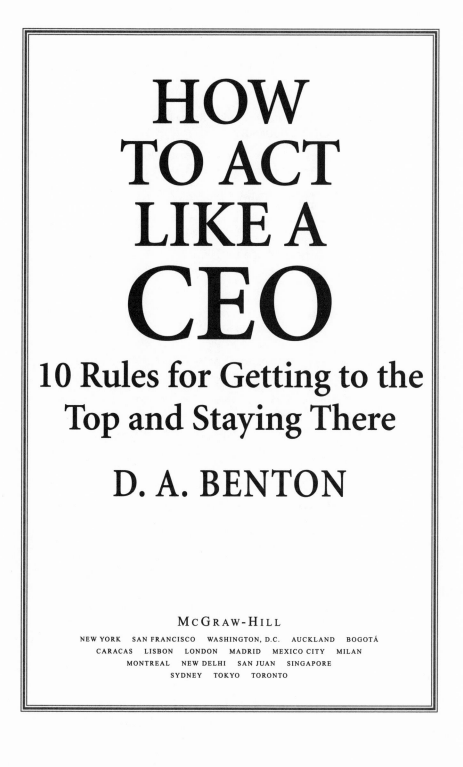

HOW
TO ACT
LIKE A
CEO

10 Rules for Getting to the Top and Staying There

D. A. BENTON

MCGRAW-HILL

NEW YORK   SAN FRANCISCO   WASHINGTON, D.C.   AUCKLAND   BOGOTÁ
CARACAS   LISBON   LONDON   MADRID   MEXICO CITY   MILAN
MONTREAL   NEW DELHI   SAN JUAN   SINGAPORE
SYDNEY   TOKYO   TORONTO

Library of Congress Cataloging-in-Publication Data

Benton, D. A. (Debra A.)
    How to act like a CEO: 10 rules for getting to the top and staying
there / D.A. Benton.
        p.   cm.
    Includes index.
    ISBN 0-07-135998-2 (alk. paper)
    1. Executive ability. 2. Executive. 3. Executive—Conduct of life.
4. Success I. Title.
    HD38.2.B4624   2000
    658.4'09—dc21   00-059457

McGraw-Hill

A Division of The McGraw-Hill Companies

1 2 3 4 5 6 7 8 9 0 AGM/AGM 0 9 8 7 6 5 4 3 2 1 0

ISBN 0-07-135998-2

It was set in New Times Roman by MM Design 2000, Inc.

Printed and bound by Quebecor World/Martinsberg.

My sincerest thanks and appreciation in completing this project goes to several people....

My husband, Rodney Sweeney, and to "Scooter".

My parents, Fred and Teresa Benton.

My agent, Mike Cohn, and editor, Mary Glenn.

And some special friends:

Amy Zach Williams, Greg and Kristie Eslick, JM Jones, Michelle Fitzhenry, Delores Doyle, Mindy Credi, Dr. Kelvin Kesler, and Konstantine Robert Buhler.

CONTENTS

THE 1000 PERCENT SOLUTION

- CEOs are different in how they can and need to act.
- You need to do what the good ones do if you want to become one yourself.

———————

"Tomorrow will be different when you wake up," says John McCains, campaign manager on the eve of the New Hampshire primary.
"You will be scrutinized like a President."
And that's the way it will go for you as you move up whatever track you are on.

Whether you're a CEO now or on your way to becoming one, you want to be a good one. No, a great one! That's wonderful. That's what is needed in the businessworld. Your employees, customers, investors, community, and competitors will demand it. But most importantly you want to be the best because that's the kind of person you are. Like California winemaker, Robert Mondavi says, "Even when I played marbles as a child, I wanted to be the best."

You are who I like to work with. You have basic ambition, drive, and talent. You'll put the effort in, and you'll make a difference in the world for all the people around you. You'll be what Super bowl Champion Denver Broncos coach, Mike Shanahan, wants on his team, "A difference maker."

"Some people grow up with a certain hunger to excel. They aren't always sure what form that hunger will take. Whether they will end up in law, business, acting, or racecar driving. But they develop a desire to excel and succeed and through sheer hard work and continuous improvement get there," says Ed Liddy, CEO of Allstate. "If you're in business it helps if you're fortunate to work for a great CEO. Then be watchful and observe what works and doesn't work. And be open to modify your style. But be careful who you hang around with."

Truth is, as good as you are now you probably could do about 1000 percent more than you thought you could. And you can do it starting today. "Some CEOs think the day they become CEO is the high point of their career. They ought to feel they're just beginning," says Jack Welch, CEO of General Electric. And really, every day you *are* beginning anew and what is required to be the best *today* is to beat the best.

Being ambitious, you (and I) pretty much have to make one of two choices in our quest for career goals. Either to

- *Run.*
- Or, *run faster*—and more efficiently.

A web-based start-up CEO says, "It's like you pass the finish line of the marathon and people say, 'Thanks a lot, but you still gotta run.'" And as Gabrielle Saveri writes in Business Week, "So they take a deep breath, another step, and don't even think about stopping."

Your race to become a champion has started if you've come far enough in your career to be interested in reading this book. You're likely described as "a very strong contributor where people have a

belief that you can 'get things done' and you enable others to also."
You may or may not be the CEO of your company *right now* but you
are the CEO of your job and your family (well maybe co-CEO). As
good as you are, wherever you are, you could still improve 1000
percent more I bet! So how, you ask....

Well I wanted to know too. I've experienced some success.
Maybe not as much as a lot of you reading this but considering what
I've been given in life I've done pretty well. *But not enough.* Like
you, I want to do more. Not so I *get* more but so that I don't waste
what I was given.

You likely have heard the sentiment from the late President John
F. Kennedy that much is expected from those to whom much is
given. And I believe that.

He wasn't alone in his thinking. I can't ever recall talking with a
CEO anywhere in the world who chooses to sit back and pronounce,
"*Now,* I have made it. I no longer have to put out effort. I can stop
trying." Or to echo a popular movie, "I'm the king of the world."
No. The good ones, the ones you and I like to be around, would
never say that.

Every CEO I've talked to, and there have been a lot, feel the skyscraper they are on top of just gives them a better view of the next
building. Not necessarily in terms of more money, power, title, but
in terms of more challenge and personal growth. After all, what else
is there to life than fighting the never-ending battle against giv-
ing-up, giving-in, and losing-out?

In my years of consulting to companies and executives around the
world I've found there are two things necessary to improve

• Hard work on your part

• The *right* hard work which is learned from the successful people
  already doing it

HARD WORK

There is no denying that the oldest "secret in the book" to success is hard work. One CEO put it simply, "In my early years I did whatever anyone asked of me and ten times more. Unfortunately, I haven't been able to let up like I thought I could."

You and I must continuously build up our *skills and experience* in the never-ending fight against laziness by putting the extra effort into our work. It takes steady, reliable, disciplined effort over time. We are not talking here about the Italian expression loosely translated that says, "I come when the cake is all made and I put the cherry on top."

Hard work requires passion—that is, a deep affinity and a deep affection—for what you're doing, for the sake of doing it. If your drive is to mainly make money you won't inspire, lead, or motivate the way you'll need to. Now you may make money but you had best invest it so you have it for your future because without the passion, you won't have followers to help you continue to make it. The CEOs I'm writing about, who *add value* to society have passion. "The CEO for the millennium has a deep passion for people and the organization," says Steve Milovich, chief people officer for Walker Digital West. "Passion is putting your mission in your heart not on your wall. It's moving it off the sheet of paper into your inside."

> *"If you don't wake up at 3 a.m. and want to do your work you're wasting your time, "*
> —Harold Edgerton
> (slow motion photographer)

If you think you'll just dabble in this extra effort stuff, you're making a mistake. To compete you have to jump in and kick like heck to do and learn all you can or else you'll very quickly discover that, "Learning a little every day soon puts you far behind whoever is learning a lot every day," as writer Asleigh Brilliants puts it. Even one day without doing extra is gone forever.

Every day that you aren't getting stronger and better, you're getting weaker and worse.

Sometimes older people look at younger people who've struck it rich, say, in the Internet world, like they haven't worked hard enough yet to achieve such financial success. Wrong. *Any success* involves hard work—those 28-year-old multimillionaires also just had some good luck and timing along with their hard work.

I received an e-mail message from one young CEO who knew I was trying to reach him. "I'm usually in my midtown New York office from 10 a.m. until the next day where around 7 or 8 a.m. I run home to shower and change and get back to the office. In otherwords I don't sleep. Being a young, hungry, entrepreneur especially in an environment that presents so many opportunities, I don't feel I can afford to miss anything," wrote Glen McCall, CEO of Global Venture Associates. He also gave me his COO's phone number "that I could use 24 hours a day to reach him too".

(Some say CEOs and CEO wannabees aren't normal. "They," say good CEOs, don't want it easy or simple but always want difficult problems and more complicated work. I've even heard the word "maniacal". Hmm. "They" may be right. But so!?)

Let me insert a side note to the e-commerce kazillionaires who are reading this book. You, who might have dreamed up or invented something, took it public, and now in your twenties or thirties have *made it* financially—or are on the verge. It's good to remember the thinking of the late Greek tycoon, Aristotle Onassis, who said, "After you reach a certain point, money becomes unimportant. What matters is success."

Whether you achieve exorbitant wealth or not, the race is not over. You're just guaranteed the ability to afford good running shoes for the rest of your life. The race *to create or build a dream, bond with and lead a group of driven human beings* is where the challenge is. Every time I ask a seasoned (nice word for an older person) executive, "What do you know now that you wish you had known 20 years ago?" The answer *always* reflects some aspect of dealing with fellow human beings. (Now a lot of them also say they wish they'd known the significance of technology 20 years ago but the first response is always about the people.)

Regardless of your age or job level, as good as you are, *get better.* That's what the good ones do. But get better in the right areas. Those areas are what you will find in this book. But first, I reiterate. *The best work on getting better every day.*

Professional football players have practice and scrimmage all week long between Sunday games. Opera and rock musicians rehearse and practice their choreography for their performance every day. Newsweek magazine wrote about Tiger Woods, "As good as he was, he's gotten that much better." Pros in every field work on getting better but in business too often we just "go with the flow" instead of seeing the next job up, all the way to the top, requires similar practice.

Bill FitzPatrick writes in *100 Action Principles of the Shaolin,* "Many people only work up to expectations. Some work just hard enough to not get fired. Some people actually work as little as half the time they are at work. These people create a window of opportunity for you to succeed. Don't worry about being obligated to work more hours to beat the competition. You probably don't have to. Instead, if you commit to working all the time you are at work, you will probably come out well ahead of your competition."

I, like you, *really* do want to be a better individual on every level. Sometimes it's blurry though to decide where to put my emphasis today and then every day after that. Again, that's why I went to the source. To find out. You see I'm a big believer in getting mentored by the best—whether or not they know they are doing it is insignificant. What counts is that I pay attention and then take action.

So you have to work hard, but you have to work on the right stuff. How do you find out the right stuff? By experiencing it through trial and error yourself, which will take a career lifetime, or go talk to the people already successfully doing it. Then take on the best actions from them. That's what I chose to do in this book.

MY—AND YOUR—MENTORS

I swear by mentoring, both giving and receiving.

Some people let the word "mentor" bother them, thinking it is for junior people. If it bothers you, use "outside confidant" instead. You can even call them "grays" or "virtual grays"—but call them.

Whatever, and whenever, you call them, make sure they are *all-stars* who are better in some area(s) than you. Your current job demands are great and will only became greater, so you don't have time to go out and "try out" a lot of people. Be careful and get some good ones. Then ask them for advice; ask them to be frank, candid and direct—and always to push you.

"Nothing makes me madder than being called a maverick who is unwilling to listen to more experienced board members. I just choose who I listen to. I've built my entire career on the philosophy of mentoring. I just *choose* my mentors very carefully," says Mike Moniz, CEO of VR.1.

"I've been fortunate in life because I've had great mentors," says John Bianchi, CEO of Frontier Gunleather. "They all had values and style. I looked up to them because they had the qualities I admire." Good mentoring means learning from the best. This book is one more mentor for you.

A good mentor is anchored with similar values but not necessarily similar perspectives.

(Note: A real bonus of utilizing mentors well is that it takes away from the loneliness factor at the top—both yours and theirs.)

"Learn from others. Find a mentor. Find two mentors. Study them. Observe their good qualities and their bad qualities. What makes them effective? What trips them up? Absorb the lessons," says Dan Burnham, CEO of Raytheon.

You want mentors from several walks of life that way you'll get "intellectual diversity". You want mentors from diverse geographic areas too. Mentoring with people close to you can result in tight lips whereas people in a different state or country will be more open. The people in your mentor loop should include the 57-year-old gray-haired-wisdom-filled curmudgeons and the 24-year-old technology whizzes.

As you read this book, you'll notice the diverse group of CEOs I chose to interview. The chiefs come from a broad group: Dow Chemical, Allstate, Ingersoll-Rand, Colgate, Myway.com, America Inc., FileNET, Coors, e-merging technologies, Open Pantry, and Frontier Gunleather—different in industry type and sizes of organizations— but not different in terms of passion and hard work from the CEO. The list was selected so it would have great diversity in industries, sizes of companies, geographic locations, and backgrounds of individuals. If you were to meet any of the people I interviewed, you would see immediately that I chose that person because of his or her integrity, leadership, creativity, financial acumen, personal power, and being a genuinely "good" person. The type you and I like to be around.

I reiterate, don't mistakenly think this advice is from the "thick waistline, thin hairline" crowd. It is the 24-, 42-, and 74-year-old CEOs who hunger for new technologies, master new situations quickly, and who build enterprises for the future. And whether they have 50,000, 5,000, or 50 employees, they don't vary in their desire to constantly better themselves. It is one of the common bonds among these pretty great CEOs. Each tries to perform better every day.

To be the best, learn from the best. That is what you'll get in this book. In the time it takes to read these 180 some pages you'll be mentored by the "best" in their field and save 8 to 16 precious years of experimenting on your own to be an exceptional player.

Besides, it's fun to see how others do it well. "I like to take advice from people who live a life I'd like to live," says Joyce Scott, CEO of Strategy Consultants Corsortium.

I set out to find those mentors for me, and for you, so I could leam to do more, better. I didn't try to learn from them so I could copy them. That would probably be impossible and definitely be stupid. Today, more than any time in life's existence, fresh thinking and quick action is a basic requirement for success. Regardless of their experiences (and there was *plenty* of variety) there was consistency in how they performed certain actions of the job.

I distilled the conversations to the important things I heard them say over and over. Many times I'll share specific quotes with you from those conversations. Sometimes I'll just say "says one CEO". The reason is that I appreciate their willingness to talk to me and I respect them as individuals. If a quote was interesting but not necessarily something they wanted attributed to them I chose to make it anonymous. All of the advice came from someone I interviewed but I tried to avoid tedium over always using names, which sometimes gets in the way of flow.

WHAT I LEARNED THAT YOU AND I CAN BOTH BENEFIT FROM

From the different worlds come the fundamentals. And whatever your age or stage in life, it's an uphill fight if you don't start work with the right fundamentals.

(Note: Fundamentals does not mean basic or simplistic; it means the necessities.)

From the fundamentals you can adapt, improvise, and learn as you go to do what's best for the situation and the time. The purpose of the fundamentals is to prepare you for whatever you will be called upon to do. Because you see, that is what *will* happen. You will be responsible for surprises for which there is no (or little) preparation. If you fail any of it, you've failed it all. So you and I will rely on developing skill in these "essential areas" and then we can use "free thinking" to add value.

Every CEO's job requires some comparable elements to execute it effectively. The lexicon which you've repeatedly heard in conversations with colleagues: *integrity, vision, strategy, operations, people skills, financial acumen, leadership, salesmanship, social responsibility, and personal balance.* It's sort of like sports. Each team and individual player has the same rules—the elements of the game—but the execution varies tremendously from player to player. And that's true in the sport of business; each player's performance varies.

"Elements of being a good CEO are straightforward. You do it or you don't do it well. You have it or you don't," says Stephen

Metzger, CEO, of SPC (SPecial Communities). "Your actions have to magnify what you're thinking and producing rather than subtracting from it."

Your substance—*the essential fundamentals of the job*—has to match your style—*the way you uniquely execute*—and vice versa. If your manner of execution supersedes the substance, you have a great deal.

Regardless of your present title, the elements *of the CEO job,* which we'll discuss in this book, must also become the elements of your *life.* You need to have non-negotiable integrity, be able to envision your future, have the approach to get there, manage the plans, deal with all kinds of people, stay financially solvent, display leadership, constantly influence and persuade, be a part of a community, and sustain some balance for personal sanity. In terms of professional and personal application those key areas make up the chapters in this book.

Good CEOs know a lot. Sometimes they act modestly act like it's not a big deal but it is. In fact things obvious to them can be a blazing revelation to others. The task is in sorting out what they know into simple, workable advice. To act like the best CEOs act out there, I condensed what they have to say into *10 CEO rules* to help you on your trip to the top. You—tomorrow's CEOs—should have these 10 rules tattooed onto your forearm, to adhere to and work on improving every day of your life

- Be yourself, unless you're a jerk (integrity—Chapter 1).
- See around corners (vision—Chapter 2).
- Make dust or eat dust (strategic planning—Chapter 3).
- Make the big play (operations—Chapter 4).
- Keep good company (people—Chapter 5).

- Be the number one fundraiser and fund protector (money—Chapter 6).
- Act like a good CEO even when you don't feel like it (leadership—Chapter 7).
- Evangelize the world (sell—Chapter 8).
- Go big or go home (social citizen—Chapter 9).
- Cut through the crap (balance —Chapter 10).

Utilizing these actions results in a comfortable, competent, confident chief—one who would make a statement like the following, "Yes, I am the company president. I am comfortable in my position and confident that I know what I am doing. You can trust me. And I want you to know I trust you and I like you. I do not know everything, but I am confident that together we will find the right answers."

So let's go forward to find the right answers *for you.*

I want you to read this book feeling like you are sitting on the back porch (or more likely the deck of a sailboat) in a conversational exchange with a bunch of CEOs. You are part of their inner circle hashing out the CEO job. Trading war stories, and offering helpful information that will make the difference in *your* own life.

So let's get to it—it's a good day for you to go kick some derriere.

Debra A. Benton
President
Benton Management Resources, Inc.
Fort Collins, Colorado

CHAPTER 1

BE YOURSELF, UNLESS YOU'RE A JERK

♦ Why integrity is so important.
♦ How to improve yours.
♦ The test—a crisis.

---

*My parents had always drummed into me that all you
have in life is your reputation; you may be very rich
but if you lose your good name, then you'll never be
happy.*
— Richard Branson
CEO of Virgin Group, Ltd.

Most everyone says integrity is "rule number one" in acting like
the best CEOs—more so than being a brilliant individual, a visionary, or a leader. *Personal integrity is the cost of entry to this position.* That's right: *How* you do your work is more important than
what your work is.

Everyone can nod his or her head and claim, "Oh yeah, I'm definitely a good citizen." But are we moral, upright, principled, honest, proper, decent, virtuous, straightforward, high-minded, noble,

kind, considerate, and fair all of the time with everyone? Pretty tough standard. Yet it is the standard to which you can aspire. If you can't, who will? And if you do, you just might set a model of excellence for those around you. The least of it is you will "sleep like a baby" (that being a healthy baby, not a colicky baby!) feeling good about yourself. And it will get you some percents on that 1000 percent more a day goal!

One month after getting the CEO job I was the most popular guy in town. It takes some guys ten years to realize that everyone patting them on the back is because of their position, not themselves.
— Dan Amos
CEO, Aflac

Regardless of your job title, this good character stuff is for everyone *at any level* in the organization so people "pat you on the back" based on who you are not what you are. Obviously, the best CEOs have the best "makeup" long before they get into the CEO position—that's partially how they got there. They practice it, not just praise it.

Good character is an evolving quality based on early values that you were exposed to along with what finally sticks in your consciousness. The result is an internal alarm system that goes off when you are crossing the line between right and wrong.

I've always tried to live by looking at "what is the right thing to do here?" It's not right, no matter how attractive it appears in the short term, if it's not the best thing to do.
— Nimish Mehta
CEO, Impresse

What's "right" is relative to your own system of values—your own exposure. It's perceptual. Other people's character, although formed the same way yours was, may end up with different boundary lines to set off their "alarm" at different times. For instance, members of the Mob have different boundary lines than the Dalai Lama. Consequently, both are going to view issues differently and choose different actions. But in general, the Western perspective is fairly homogenized as to what is right and wrong.

(Several CEOs said to me, "I think, 'How do I want to read about this on the front page of *The Wall Street Journal*'; that shapes right or wrong pretty quickly.")

You must have a tolerance for varying perspectives. But an intolerance for what is considered irreprehensible.
— Rev. Jim Forbes
Senior Minister, Riversi Cathedral

You set your own standard of behavior. Live it consistently. Teach it to those who want to follow the same standard. And understand that not everyone is exactly like you. In reality, their "view" can be different from your "view" while both of you pledge you are acting "right or wrong."

Sometimes people think the arena with the *least* ethics is politics. I asked Rick O'Donnell, Director, Governors Office of Policy and Initiatives for Colorado Governor Bill Owens, about it.

Politics is a microcosm of population. There is not a higher percent of bad people in politics. They are just exposed. If a CEO says he's going to go in a certain direction then a year later it didn't happen that way, no one knows unless it's mentioned in the annual report. Whereas, if a politician says something the media is going to remember. The politician is scrutinized every time he changes his mind simply because people see it. The fact is people grow and change their mind regardless of their work.

3

Integrity is not as black and white as you'd like it to be. Particularly when you add the diversity of today's workforce where different cultures, religions, history, and exposure all affect the makeup. In other words, you can't be judgmental about your "right" being more "right." They just may feel the same about you.

So you average it out: *on balance*, you act—and make—decisions *not* just for your good but *for the common good*. You sacrifice your own aspirations for the common good. You decide to act like *integrity is nonnegotiable* while, at the same time, tolerantly understand that people view the same truth differently. You choose to be *credible beyond reproach* and accept that others try to also. You act this way not just to do things in a legal manner but because it's your private code of behavior. And you *consistently* follow through on these beliefs all of the time even during times of crisis. You are the kind of person who will be a good CEO like these four have a reputation for being.

Integrity is a supreme requirement. And I consider trust to be the greatest motivator.
— Bob Galvin
Chairman of Motorola's
executive committee

And trust takes a lot of moxie and commitment to build. It takes a long time, and you can lose it overnight.
— Max Depree
Former Chairman of Herman Miller

I think there are two essential things. The first is the value of people, the second is the importance of values.
— Bob Haas
CEO, Levi Strauss

Ethics are an invaluable intangible that each successful leader bases their actions on. One of the things that my firm prides itself on is the ethical values that run deep in our blood. It's something that is worn on our sleeves. We look to our core values in hiring, client selection, and everyday decisions. Even our firm by-line is: "ethics fed brainware." Ethics is something that has been deeply seeded in all successful organizations and their leaders and will continue to be for as long as successful business will exist.

> — Brian McCune
> Managing Partner,
> e-merging technologies group

Although it might be obvious that integrity is rule number one, let me reinforce that conclusion with reasons why it is.

It's a basic requirement for leadership

People follow you because of your character, not your job title. "A really good way to lose leadership is to be thought of as having lost integrity," says Curt Carter, CEO of Gulbransen, Inc. and America, Inc. "CEOs jealously guard their good name. They'll pay ransom for their good name—like paying a bill they don't owe."

General Schwarzkoff says leadership boils down to competence and character, and more often the differentiator is character.

(Throughout this entire book you'll read that every aspect of the CEO's job is fundamentally guided by his or her character regardless of industry, size, or anything else.)

Ethical behavior turns out to be the easiest to do

When you have an "unwavering constitution," you can be yourself and not work so hard trying to be something you aren't. You don't run the risk of people discovering artifice. Like you've heard people say, it's so much easier to tell the truth; then I don't have to try to remember all my lies.

5

When you try to "do right," it alleviates stress of decisions. It softens setbacks and disappointments. It takes care of ingratitude. And it turns out to be a good business strategy because nothing baffles someone full of tricks and lies more than simple, straightforward integrity.

People sense when you are guided by deeply held values or when you aren't *and* they sense when you aren't but act like you are.

"The first things our parents taught us about right and wrong are true. They still work even in the complexity of today's business," says Nancy May, CEO of The Women's Global Business Alliance.

Sets standard of expectation

People mirror those around them. Your people are a reflection of you. If you dip your toes in the pool of nonethical behavior, even a little, it starts a whirlpool. "The CEO needs to be the personification of the company's values to his organization, customers, suppliers, and outside world," says Daryl Brewster, President of Planters Specialty Foods. "It's that simple."

When the elephant sneezes, everybody catches a cold. (Gross expression, huh?) But you get it, everything gets passed around.

"The CEO is a role model, his major responsibility is to bring honesty and openness into it but it has to be his own personality. I had high standards and felt if I set the example people would live up to them and the company would benefit greatly," says Duane Pearsall, retired CEO of Columbine Venture Capital. "I had an individual that I wanted to promote. He was bright, energetic, a good thinker, did an outstanding job but he had a character flaw he couldn't get over. I tried to help and sometimes he did better. But he couldn't quite make it. So I ended up not promoting him."

You truly demonstrate and prove your integrity in *your actions*. One small example is that you have to do what you'd expect your people to do: "When I was visiting the field I'd schedule a flight home at 6:00 p.m. so I could work with my people until 5:00 p.m. If I expect a full day from them they have to see me do the same. You either live by the rules or don't live by the rules," says Paul Schlossberg, CEO of D/FW Consulting. And sometimes you have to *inconvenience* yourself to remain that "person with integrity." If your people can't spend more than $150 a night for a hotel room than you can't either. Play by the rules, whatever they are.

If you provide a constant example and application, *that* will run the company when you aren't there to tell people what to do. That becomes part of your corporate culture.

"The person I believe is the executive secretary," says Nancy Albertini, CEO of Taylor-Winfield. We had a phone call from a CEO who wanted us to do a search for him. I returned the call. His secretary semisnarled, 'who are you, what are you calling about, and he's too busy to talk to you.' I just said, 'Fine. Just explain to him why he hasn't heard back from me was because you explained he was too busy to talk to me.' Well the man did call back and was overly pleasant to me because he needed me to do the search. When I started to work with him I discovered that his manner was to be nice when it served him and not to be the rest of the time. It only reinforced my commitment to paying attention to the CEO's secretary. If she is nice and helpful it tells me about his management style. If she isn't, that tells me something too. I make sure in my own office that everyone treats anyone who calls like they are the Queen of England."

Creates and leaves a legacy

You can't always bet on technology, can't bet on the numbers, and can't bet on the economy. What you can bet on at the end of the day is management. People track your performance.

It's called your reputation while you're here and your legacy when you're gone.

The way to gain a reputation is to endeavor to be what you desire to appear.
— Socrates

People see through you when you aren't honest and ethical— either right away or eventually. The truth will come out. You can't misstate. You can't shape the truth a little. You can't even be coy. There is no exit. Eventually, you'll be faced with the facts. Again, that creates your legacy.

Pick your guiding principles and apply them religiously to hiring, building an organization, or dealing with customers. Even in the exploding technology world where anything goes, you can't risk betraying other employees or businesses. It will come back to haunt you eventually.

Evidence over time creates your reputation and legacy. "Previous integrity. That's your road map to follow when evaluating someone," says Lawrence Land, attorney-at-law.

Talk about legacy! "I'd rather have a 'handshake deal' with a person of integrity, than a forty page document with a person who embraces a 'Clintonesque' personality," says Dave Powelson, CEO of TRI-R Systems.

It pays off financially

"I've always put principle before profit," says John Bianchi, CEO of Frontier Gunleather. "Principles in the short term guarantee profits in the long term."

Sure, I know it's not always financially rewarding to do what's right. It's not easy to be the person you'd like to be or as one person put it, "the person my dog thinks I am."

You will easily find ways to cut costs and increase the bottom line but you can also end up cutting into your principles. Perhaps the financial payoff is that you *stay* in business with a good reputation.

"We had consultants reviewing our business several times over the years and they'd always report that 'You are overstaffed.' We did hire too much help and that costs us. But that followed our two guiding principles: provide quality care and put what was best for our patients first. Our pay was self-satisfaction," says Dr. Kelvin Kesler, Chief of Ft. Collins Women's Clinic.

It keeps you out of jail

People choose to do the right thing because it fits their self-image or they fear temporal or spiritual punishment. It's like the line in the old movie *Rogue River*, "Every man is a potential criminal, only fear stops him."

The fact is, the higher you go up, the more freedom and power you have. With that comes self-pride in accomplishment and feeling good about what you've done. That's all good and normal. When taken to the extreme, it becomes bad. Extreme means "I'm special, I'm different, the same rules no longer apply to me. I have a right to get away with more—just look at who I am." This kind of look-down-your-nose-superiority may work in Hollywood but not in the real world.

It is probably the nature of people to do what they can get away with. Comedienne Chris Rock puts it, "A man is basically as faithful as his options." And at the top of the skyscraper, you can get away with more. But don't. It's back to your standard every day. You get more options (mental and monetary) as CEO. Be careful how you take them. You can go to jail.

Michael Wise, CEO for the former Silverado Banking who was sentenced to 3-years in a federal prison camp after pleading guilty to stealing $8.75 million from investors is quoted in the *Denver Post*, "I've been blessed, with a lot of talent and people who trusted me...I misused both of them."

Do not give yourself the permission to be even a little questionable– despite the option to do so. As some historian put it, "Empires cracked before they crumbled. Even when the first cracks seemed easily mended."

Good people will be willing to work with you

In business, we generally have options in terms of whom we choose to do business with. "If I'm dealing with someone I sense lacks integrity, I distance myself quickly. If they work for me they don't last long. Integrity is fundamental to our corporate culture," says Ted Wright, CEO of Ampersand.

Does it take longer than a second to answer whether, if given a choice, you'd work for someone who demonstrates integrity over someone questionable? Well, the same goes for who would work for you.

> *If the boss' motive, character, and ability are something you don't respect, quit. If you have a subordinate who has a motive, character, or ability you can't accept, fire him or her.*
> — Curt Carter, 'Carter's Law'
> CEO Gulbransen Inc. and America Inc.

There was a sign on one publisher's wall for years, "We rip off the other guy and pass the savings on to you." Now do you think that was a successful recruiting poster?

This is a biggee. If you don't have good people working for you, you will fail despite your effort, intelligence, actions, etc. Good people don't work for bad bosses (at least not for long). If you are a boss who's experienced recent success and you think you "hold a hot hand" and can therefore slip and slide a little because of your "power," you will eventually find out differently.

Power comes from integrity

Power is duty that comes from integrity.

The truth is that at the CEO level there are many opportunities to do wrong. The CEO has a very long leash. There's little scrutiny above that level in many business situations.

And when you clearly have the option—but choose not to take it—you have personal power because of how you handled yourself and people will see, understand, and respond accordingly.

We like movies with some version of a hero overcoming a hurdle—a time where he could lie, cheat, or steal—but instead he ends up more powerful because of not doing it. Well, that opportunity comes to you every day to be a hero at the office.

"People felt I'd be fair and compassionate. And I got devoted employees because of it. I didn't need to worry about standing in the doorway at 5:00 and be trampled by exiting employees," says Dr. Kelvin Kesler, Chief of Ft. Collins Women's Clinic.

(*Author's Note*: Throughout this chapter, I've pretty liberally interchanged words here such as integrity, ethics, character, values, and honesty. I know the dictionary definition is different for each but I'm going to continue interchanging them because you get my point when I use them that it's all about being a good person. I could even add moral, trustworthy, upright, authentic, sincere, and "does the right thing." Whatever word you choose to use is fine—to describe right or wrong—as long as you never try to fool yourself.

You have to be truly true to yourself. As the CEO, no matter how hard you try, you won't please everyone and some will feel you lack integrity. That's a price you pay for being in the spotlight. You'll

11

have enemies. When they appear, listen to what they criticize you for. Change if they are right and be grateful for them—they help you get better.

Integrity is the goal but not always the reality.

The fact is that sometimes integrity takes a back seat to keeping a CEO going in the direction of a target. More than one CEO has stepped over a few marginal hurdles without spending 2 seconds of thought on people he's hurting. There is a lot done "in the dark, not in the public light," as one CEO put it.

He explained, "A company starts up a project, adds people, and builds up an infrastructure. Then every 3-5 years they clip it off to make it economically viable. They don't spend a lot of time thinking about the division full of people who have to relocate or the 20-year employee who's losing her job. Companies trim back and see what raises its ugly head. The goal is to gain efficiencies. To get what is good for them in the long term. They give a financial package to people of six or nine months for an early out, help to re-educate them and so forth. It's patchwork. They do it because it's demanded of them or there would be an outrage."

(But, on the one hand, you could make the case that the smaller operation was shut down for the common good of the bigger operation. It can get pretty gray out there as you can tell.)

CEOs have superordinate goals. They don't start out to *not* be ethical. But with pressure from outside sources, timing issues, things can start to slip and slide. Unfortunately, there will always be many times and many companies who do not reward integrity if it gets in the way of getting things done.

"The CEO is still a person. There is no such thing as a perfect person. A CEO may slip from time to time when he sees a chance to do something a little unethical to help make things look better to stockholders or whatever. One time I had a supplier give me a pretty valuable gift but I gave it right back to him. I didn't want to be indebted to him if things turned sour. To hell with it, do what's right, I always say," says Ernie Howell, retired president of WPM Systems. "You don't have to live with the stockholders or your employees. You stay ethical more for yourself, because you have to live with yourself.... There have always been con artists, in any field, the only difference now is that they can just communicate faster today."

I was in Japan during their worst nuclear accident in recent history. The television news carried coverage of the Japanese company president whose plant had caused the nuclear leak. He was literally on his knees in front of his employees asking for forgiveness, with the words, "We apologize from the bottom of our hearts." True, it's partially a cultural thing, but can you imagine a U.S. president on his or her knees asking for forgiveness? I don't think so!

The same television show had an interview with a U.S. company CEO who had been fired from his highly visible, big company job, and was going to head an Internet start-up. The reporter asked if his departure had been a humbling experience. He avoided the question so the reporter asked again. After being pressed to answer, all the CEO would admit was, "I do not wish to repeat the experience." Known for his arrogance while CEO, he continues it in his new venture.

These two individuals didn't start out to do anything questionable. Things happen. The best you can do is to listen when the alarm goes off in your head:

+ Every person is the architect of his or her own character.
+ Integrity—character—affects absolutely every other part of your life.

13

• It's the one thing no one can take away, and we can't lose it unless we choose to.

• This is your reality; your reputation is what others think, but this is reality.

• It's the result of your own effort and endeavors; no one gave it to you other than early exposure from parents and society.

• It's the area to work on the most for it will serve you the best (J. P. Morgan considered the best bank collateral to be "character").

• To create something of value, you must be someone of value.

I have to, and you have to, be careful not to judge—"there but for the grace of God go I" and "walk a mile in my moccasins" are expressions that have lasted for a reason. It's our responsibility to seek to understand, not judge.

However good you are, get better

As good as you are, *check on what you need to work on* to get even better. You should try to get better on every skill part of your job—try to improve the integrity side too.

It seems a little silly. You could say you have it or you don't. I know myself pretty well and I work on being the person my dog thinks I am but I also know I could be better. And in your heart I bet you feel similarly.

"Most people who attain the CEO level have values early on in their career. You can improve management skills but integrity is one thing that *has* to get stronger. At the end of the day, the other party has to believe in and trust the other party. Trust is most important with the CEO," says Larry Dickenson, senior vice president, of Boeing.

You can reinvent yourself every day (or every month or every year) as necessary. You do not have to rely on what has worked to date. *You can change frequently and still be yourself—but always a better self!*

And by changing yourself I don't mean like Dustin Hoffman quipped, "I want to be as I always envisioned myself to be: taller, smaller nose, handsome, better teeth."

Everyone needs periodic review. "As you get older you have more information about yourself and what you're good at," says John Sculley, former CEO of Apple. Don't wait until you're older, have more time, have a problem, or a "change in life." Do it now.

First you have to do a little self-reflection. If you wait until you are at the top to try to be self-reflective, you won't be able to because you've not developed the habit. Or more likely you won't want to because you don't want to "jinx what got me here" as one CEO put it. (You might want to review my book *Secrets of a CEO Coach*, McGraw-Hill, 1999; it contains 20 pages of self-reflection questions.)

Think of five important situations you've been involved with recently that turned out "just okay," not "great." Isolate each one and ask yourself:

* How could I have handled that better?
* Where did I disappoint myself a little?
* What negative impact did I have on people and what can I do about that now?
* What do I want to remember when it happens again so I handle it better?
* What can I do about it now?

Sound like beating yourself up? Wrong. Sound like a waste of time? Wrong.

I just took a recent situation that happened in my own life through these questions. What I learned about it upon self-reflection: I should have kept emotional reaction out of it. I shouldn't have listened to other parties with an "agenda". I'm a little embarrassed that others saw me "less than the image I like people to see." I now have an enemy, at least temporarily, until I fix it. In hindsight I would not have done this and instead engaged with a more open point of view with the person involved. What I want to remember next time is not to be so high and mighty about how right I was because I wasn't as right as I thought I was! And what I have to do about it now is swallow my pride and apologize.

The higher the altitude, the lower the feedback. Self-reflection is to provide your own tough feedback before you get it from others.

I, like you, hate to disappoint myself so by doing this little exercise, I've thought it through with enough intensity that I will likely not repeat it. Or if I do, I'll catch and correct earlier on. (For those curious about the situation that I didn't handle well, no, I'm not going to tell you any more!)

You can do self-reflection on your drive to the office, in between appointments, while resting after exercise, or any other time you have 5 minutes of concentrated thought to focus with.

Simply decide what's right for you. Write it down, date it, keep it. Refer to it later. (Don't turn the page and just make a mental note. Do it now. It won't take that long. You can do it again when you have more time. *Someday* is right now.)

"Every year I go off to the mountains in Utah and revisit what is important to me. I write it down. I carry it around in my briefcase, put it by my phone on my desk, share it with people I value. I 'declare' myself and basically say 'judge me' against what I say. I've done this for 10 years. It's made me grow and have more insight into myself. Every year I make revisions but I'm the same essential person. The way to authenticity is to work at understanding where you are. Network with people who help you develop insight into yourself. I use a graphologist, a retired CEO 80 years old, and some friends and family. I periodically check in with them. I'm alert to their insights. Once I declare it, I feel like the emperor with no clothes. I'm obligated to keep at it," says Doug Conant, President of Nabisco Foods Company. "I initially didn't share my goals with people but now I do. I've found it helps me live up to them."

As I wrote earlier, ethics is a word that is frequently brought up. There's the dictionary definition of the word: a principle of right or good conduct. And then there is Bill Daniels', CEO of Daniels Cablevision, working definition, "If you make a deal and it doesn't feel right chances are it's unethical." Bill, who was frequently on the business magazine's income lists of the "top 400" in the country, proudly gave me a copy of his company's code of conduct *since* 1958. Although written as the company code, I've rewritten it for a personal code:

1. I will exemplify the highest standards of honesty, integrity, and personal conduct, and adhere to all legal and ethical principles.

2. I will deal with all constituents in an honest, courteous, respectful, and polite manner.

3. I will work with all in an honest, civil manner, and will show respect to my colleagues and to their opinions.

4. I will not knowingly disseminate false or misleading information and will act promptly to correct any erroneous communications for which I am responsible.

5. I will not engage in practices which corrupt the industries I serve or damage the business community.

6. I will scrupulously safeguard the right of privacy of present, former, and prospective associates and treat information obtained in a confidential manner.

7. I will base my professional principles on the fundamental value and dignity of the individual.

8. I will take responsibility for my actions.

"Can you do business without this code of ethics?" I asked Daniels. "Yes, but not for long. Anyone who does not live up to his integrity, ethics, and character will eventually be found out. Can you learn to be better at it? The answer to that is yes."

The purpose of the self-reflection questions earlier is to give you experience in shaping your personal code. Then write it down.

A couple of chiefs let me share theirs with you:

It is my continuing resolve to be:

Financially secure and independent of outside influence.

A source of positive influence and example with those I meet.

Confident all friends will be served and cared for according to their needs and my abilities.

Vigilant that my business and personal affairs are conducted in a manner which will enrich those involved.

Balance in my business and personal goals so each will be successful and fulfilled.

> — John Krebbs
> CEO, Parker Album Company

(*Note*: When Krebbs gave me this I wanted to use it but wanted his permission to attribute it to him. "Yes, use my name, I'm proud of it. It took me five years to come up with it and I've stuck by it for twenty years.")

My mission is to raise my family, teach my children, lead my organization, be a good friend, feel good about myself, continue to grow, and help others to grow.

To be bold in my pursuits, but balance courage and consideration. To be a great companion to my wife, love her and care for her, not caretake her.

To provide a home that is loving and caring and mentors interdependence. To have good friends to share our lives with. To always keep learning. To be responsible and accountable to me first, and society second.

And finally, to live so when my children think of Fairness, Caring, and Integrity...they think of me.
— Michael Trufant,
CEO, G&M Marine Inc.

And one CEO's code of conduct was simply, "I put myself in the other person's shoes. It's my constant compass."

"We put our values down on one sheet of paper, enclose them in plastic and keep them on our desks. We eat our sandwiches on it. We post them at the workplace. And I put my support behind it. Any time we send a message that is different than on the statement people tell me about it. Some companies have strong cultures and some have weak cultures. The CEO decides which it's going to be. People want to be part of an organization with a strong culture they can commit to," says Sam Ginn, Chairman, of Vodafone Airtouch. At the Frank Russell Company, they laser their business code into a wood cube:

We value integrity, in an environment of mutual trust and respect, including fairness, teamwork, tolerance, family, and community, in our process of providing added value to our clients.

We value our associates, families and clients, who are critical to our success. We especially appreciate our associates' commitment to the Company, and in return seek to provide opportunities for them to develop.

We require honest profitability for continued success, and we reward our associates accordingly. We seek to exceed client expectations. We aspire to a higher set of values than required by law.

A code of ethics can be personal one or it can be corporate. The point is to have one that works personally and professionally for you.

Think carefully, purposefully, and seriously about what really matters to you—for your own growth and development

"A couple of weeks ago I went through a re-evaluation: where I am and what I'm doing. I found I'm extremely happy, and satisfied. I value and enjoy life and my friends, "says John Krebbs, CEO of Parker Album Company. If you're lucky, you may come up with a similar conclusion but I want you to go through the exercise to check it out. (Remember, he's one of the people who had written down a code. You're more likely to meet it if you know what it is and can refer to it on a regular basis.)

There is no separation, in my opinion, between who we are at work and who we are away from work—so work on improving both.

Conduct yourself in a manner that if whatever you say or do gets back to your wife, children, parents, grandparents, friends, parish priest, etc., you're okay with it. If you "spit up" on yourself do not hesitate to apologize to those you offended, hurt, or humiliated.

> — Ron Brown
> CEO, Maximation

Live your code: where you falter, alter

Be self-disciplined to the extreme when it comes to living your code. Any honest self-evaluation results in areas for development so do something about your weaknesses. *Where you falter, alter.*

You wouldn't be reading this book if you didn't have the goal to be better. Like a lot of things in life, it's not how talented you are, it's deciding what you want and wanting it bad enough to be self-disciplined in getting it.

Every day I get the difficult things done first thing in the morning.
— Rick Pitino
Boston Celtics coach

The ABC news show *20/20* reported on a nationwide study that determined self-control was an indicator of success. Previously it was thought that self-esteem was the key success factor. But no, it's self-discipline.

The study concluded that self-esteem comes out of self-discipline. Self esteem, like self-discipline is one of those personality traits prevalent in effective CEOs. You feel good about yourself when you've accomplished something and you accomplish something through self-discipline.

You and I both know we are more capable than we act on many occasions. If we will discipline ourselves to go further, faster, *we can* do more. A good foot racer runs *past* the finish line. When you run *through* the goal, not to it, you won't fall short of it. Like anything in life: If you go on, you win. If you stop, you lose.

The CEO test—a crisis

The real test of integrity is *when something goes wrong.* A crisis. Or, to put it nicely, a *nonroutine* situation. There is no better way to observe someone than during a crisis. If you change your integrity when times are bad, you had no integrity to begin with.

As one CEO put it, "set them to simmer and take off the scum."

A crisis is where your character really shows up. The test isn't during the good times where you're just keeping a steady helm in the storm. The behavior you exhibit during a crisis—whether you panic or cave or play a little dirty—that's what people look at as the real person.

"A crisis is when you are challenged the most. You grow the most. And you find out who you really are. How you behave at those times is as important as what you do today or every day," says Leo Kiely, CEO of Coors. "People won't work for submarine captains."

The CEO must have the ability to stay on deck while the wind is blowing at gale force.
— Thome Matisz
CEO, Solotec

People with an ethical reputation can guide others through a crisis. Those without, simply won't be trusted and therefore cannot get others to follow them to turn things around. Even as the CEO, in a crisis, you have to rely on others, put faith in others. And, those others will only be reliable if they feel *you* are reliable.

There are varying levels of crisis. From losing a major customer, to finding out the computer failed and you've gone offline, or your health insurance company goes bankrupt and in 30 days your employees will be out of coverage. (One CEO described a crisis situation he was in, "I felt like I was in deep water and was caught in a wave in a cave.")

Then there is the manufacturing plant that blows up, or the food product that was tainted or the airplane crash, or someone shoots up the workplace. ("Foxhole religion," is what Jack Falvey CEO, calls it. "Leaders have a better prayer life.")

You can't control 99 percent of the stuff in business life. There are steps to deal with in a crisis which I will lay out. The steps, although important, aren't as important as the tone and manner in which you carry them out. The mantle of integrity must pervade in every single detail in every way.

- *Take charge.* You must call the shots. You can direct a public relations person or vice president to help relay information to the media, public, shareholders, whomever—just remember you are in charge and responsible for the crisis management, not anyone else. "When things are down you have to be out in front. You're the captain, it's your problem," says Lee Roberts, FileNET

- *Choose someone to collect information.* You need to have as much available data as possible to make decisions. Few crises start at the CEO level, but rather way down the line. You don't have a lot of control but you can have lots of information.

- *Ensure the crisis is over.* The CEO usually cannot fix the problem directly and most likely doesn't even have the technical knowledge to know what needs to be done. Hopefully, the frontline workers are trained well enough and have the attitude of integrity, inspired by the CEO, to do the right thing and get the situation resolved or at least under control as efficiently and effectively as possible.

- *Assess damage.* As soon as possible review the ramifications of all parties involved.

- *Delegate who is the person to develop the recovery plan.* You want someone with integrity as we're discussing in this chapter. At this time, more than ever, you need someone who will "keep his or her head about them when others are losing theirs."

- *Be visible.* Above all, don't become paralyzed with fear about whether what you're doing is right. Go out and show concern and compassion. While the frontline troops are fixing the problem, you must be boosting their morale, comforting families, and letting everyone know that this is a leader and an organization that cares about its employees and their welfare and will be with them in a time of crisis.

That's a more formal crisis management approach but all day little ones pop up that require the CEO's intuitive creativity. If you truly trust and understand your integrity, you're able to use it in emergency situations intuitively. When your 6-year-old falls off his bicycle, you don't race to the library to pick up a book or search the net to decide what to do. You react instantly and you react intuitively.

Similar minibusiness crisis occur all day long. You don't know when one of them is going to occur and at the time you experience it you react with the right call that comes from your character. So you: (1) gather facts, (2) get your mind over the fact you'll never have enough facts, (3) take the shortest amount of time for #1 and #2, and (4) then do it—act!

One CEO gathered his legal team in a borrowed conference room, threw a key onto the center of the table, and said, "This is the key to the restroom. After we figure out this problem, who's going to do what, when's it going to be done, what will be the cost, you can have it." Two and a half hours later the plan was on the white board.

Michael Trufant, CEO of G&M Marine Inc., offered his five-step approach to dealing with a "test":

1. Keep your head when others are losing theirs (credited to Kipling).
2. Be strategic, unless the building is on fire, and take the time to think beyond the first steps and consider the good and bad consequences of action.
3. Maintain a broad perspective over time versus looking at an "event" in time. (Something he learned from his father.)
4. Have faith and do the right thing which is usually the easiest to know, yet often hard to do.
5. Communicate well: keep a cool head, think strategically, keep perspective, decide on the right thing to do...and communicate all of this to those to whom it is important and relevant to know.

Craig Watson, Vice President of FMC, says, "I like the Marine Corps definition of integrity: doing the right thing when no one's looking. Then when a crisis hits—something that tests whether you believe the end justifies the means—you're face-to-face with your values that you're supposed to hold sacrosanct. Some additional steps: (1) since you understand your deeply held values, (2) use this understanding to rank order what's important in a given situation, (3) if you have to give something up in the process of dealing with a crisis, start at the bottom of the list."

For life to be meaningful you must have a challenge. It feels satisfying to overcome a crisis and it gives you strength for the next time.

Sometimes you're going to lose.

Regardless of preparation, effort, and good intent, you don't always achieve the outcome you desire. That's another crisis, when you lose.

For most CEOs if you aren't winning, you're miserable. And it's little consolation that losing makes you better. But it does. Losing is

* Nothing but education

* The first step to something better

* Closer to victory the next time…if you turn up the 1000 percent effort

And besides "winning" is easy and you don't need easy!

You can temporarily feel a little sad about things not working as you hoped. But you just keep going. That's another test of integrity, when you get knocked down, do you get back up? Again, and again, and again, as necessary? "I remember a guy I counted on who was corrupt. I can still see him as he drove out of town in a yellow Porsche owing $90,000 in unpaid bills that I had to pay," says one CEO. "Yeah, I feel a little sad about that but we had to keep going."

Terry Bradshaw asked John Elway, former quarterback for the Denver Broncos, if he learned more from his losses or his wins. "Losing the Super Bowls made me mentally tougher and makes the win that much more special." As another sports legend put it, Rick Pitino, "Losing is fertilizer for my growth."

We know that but it still is miserable while it's happening.

"I had set up a $48 million contract with Moscow. It was 2 years of effort, building trust and getting to know the right people. I had the solution to their problem. My partner in the deal came over for the final meeting. He blew it. Two years worth of work wiped out," says Jim McBride, CEO of ATMO. "I took him to the airport to send him home the next morning at 5 a.m. I admit, I was totally inebriated. The taxi driver looked at me and said 'you start somewhat early for an American.' If you just lost $48 million wouldn't you get drunk?" I said, "Yeah, I guess so," he said.

How you lose is another test of character. So when you have a setback, crisis, or a failure, don't be a jerk:

♦ Don't be overly convinced of your own importance.

♦ Don't think you are the "exception to the rule" in doing whatever you feel like.

♦ Don't act only to please yourself.

♦ Don't break your word.

♦ Don't be dishonest.[1]

♦ Don't be mean or nasty.

♦ Don't kick people in the face anywhere along the way.

♦ Don't yell and scream.

♦ Don't embarrass others.

♦ Don't turn supporters into road kill when the going gets tough.

♦ Don't be arrogant no matter how much of a right you think you have to be arrogant.

♦ Don't get good at being bad.

---

[1]Did you know you can go to jail for these dishonest acts:
-5 years: For exaggerating your symptoms to a doctor so that your insurance company will pay for a checkup it wouldn't otherwise cover.
-10 years: For taking a confidential list of your firm's clients and their phone numbers with you to a new job.
-1 year: For copying a friend's computer game instead of buying it yourself.
-5 years: For eavesdropping on your neighbor's cordless phone conversation and then gossip about what you heard.

If you follow these steps, you still might make it to the top but it cuts your shelf life down in staying there. And you better have *very* good people who mend a lot of fences for you.

Addressing 800 lawyers at the Waldorf Astoria, Jerry Spence said, "Don't act like me. Don't act like someone you know. Be yourself, unless you're an asshole." (All I can say is, pretty good advice!)

Final advice on integrity: Exceed other's expectations.

When wealth is lost, nothing is lost; when health is lost, something is lost; when character is lost, all is lost.
                                        — German motto

CHAPTER 2

SEE AROUND CORNERS

♦ Vision is....
♦ How to improve yours.
♦ Now, change it.

_____

Every day I spend at work I have one eye on the future. It's part of the lens I use to look at the world."

— Doug Conant
President, Nabisco Foods Group

What sets CEOs apart, and consequently their organizations, is their vision. It's the magic. The possibilities of tomorrow—the big, hairy, audacious ideas about how things *could* come together if certain things happen...."You have to be able to imagine a future state. That's a critical component to anything you do in life. Whether in a big or small company. And you have to be able to articulate it. You can't get there alone. You need a vision that gives people something to shoot for. Its like the old story of two bricklayers, when asked, one says he is building a wall, the other says he is building a cathedral," says Bill Stavropoulos, CEO of The Dow Chemical Company.

In today's wild economy if you can't quickly see paths ahead, you won't inspire (or retain) quality people and without quality people you won't get investors or customers and you won't be able to follow your dreams.

Creativity and innovation are the only true weapons in the fight for differentiation.
— Christopher Day
Co-president, Packtion Corporation

"Do you want to spend the rest of your life selling sugared water, or do you want a chance to change the world?" were the words Steve Jobs' used to persuade John Sculley to leave Pepsi for Apple. Jobs was selling a vision he hoped would attract Sculley. It worked. It later turned out to be a bad decision for both of them but that's a different book.

This is an area where you can really make your mark. When Bill Gates turned the daily responsibility of running Microsoft to Steve Ballmer, he made a sweeping change in the organization. Ballmer called it "Vision: Version 2" and whether it was to pre-empt an antitrust breakup or not, it divided the company into eight parts and charted a new direction for the organization. Ballmer also publicly declared the vision from now on was for Microsoft "to delight" it's customers.

"Vision, to be meaningful, must clearly lead to some significant (it helps if it is also dramatic) outcome or change. Otherwise you will lack impact and it will be very hard to capture people's imagination to facilitate achieving this vision," says Larry Kopp, venture capitalist.

Vision in itself isn't a moneymaker but it leads profit and it's a major component to execute strategy. "Vision is the quarterback who sees daylight," says Jeff Cunningham, Chairman, iLIFE.com.

Vision is too fancy, but you have to have a dream.
— Warren Buffet
Chairman, Berkshire Hathaway

The chairman and CEO of Nieman Marcus says, "Many of us tend to think of vision as a rarefied ability, something unique to individuals of a creative or intellectual bent. Artists have vision. And inventors. And also presidents. But the fact is, all of us have it— every time we imagine the future, every time we feel hope, every time we 'dream things that never were and ask Why not?' Think of someone whose vision has impacted your life. The colleague who chose to take the road less traveled because of unknown possibilities. That special teacher who encouraged you to reach for your dreams. Or maybe your parents, who believed you could do anything. That's vision. It has almost nothing to do with the eyes, and everything to do with the mind."

The "dream" gets turned into the company mission, a direction, a massive goal, or the annual objectives—whatever you choose to call it.

If you haven't already started being visionary, start now.

You don't "get it" once you become CEO. It comes from a lifetime of practice.

And it's okay to start the vision work small and *expand* it with success. It won't expand much with failure! It's like if you cross a street and break your leg getting hit by a bus you won't be crossing another street for a while. But if you strategically make it across the street safely, you might cross another one. The same is true of developing "vision." Start small, as you succeed, go bigger.

31

Defining your vision is like going on an adventure. It's a difficult assignment and consequently a challenge. There are unknown aspects and therefore a high risk. And there is potential for great reward.

— Jack Linkletter
CEO, Linkletter Enterprises

You can start now and you can start small—regardless of what level you are in the organization. First, decide to make a proactive commitment to be future oriented. Second, get a whole bunch of information from diverse places and start processing it.

Assess where you are

Review what you've already been doing well—your core competencies—and where there is opportunity to be and do more. Wynn Williard, President of Planters Ltd., says, "Ask what do we have that they (the customer) don't know they need."

While the visionary foresees the future they also "stick to their knitting" as the expression goes. "At John-Manville we have always been in the building materials business. Many years ago, before I was here we got into golf cart manufacturing. Then we got into the sprinkler business. Then we got into the resort business. Then we got into trouble. We were so far away from our core business," says CEO Jerry Henry, CEO, John-Manville Corporation.

"A visionary perspective is like a pyramid. At the top your eyes need to see out farthest," says Curt Carter, CEO of Gulbransen Inc., and America Inc.

Fantasize a little about where you could be

In the beginning base it on beliefs, gut feeling, goals, and dreams. You can switch to reality later.

Jeffrey Hoffman, co-founder of priceline.com and CEO of Priceline Perfect YardSale, says they start out every vision conversation with "'wouldn't it be cool if...' And 'if you could start it over what would you do about....' We forget reality for a while. We start in utopia and go back to reality."

Think big goals. Aim big. A "piece" of big will be bigger than a "piece" of small. It's more exciting to the team if it's big and audacious. "Set superordinate goals," says George Russell, Chairman, of the Frank Russell Company. "Otherwise you are not likely to make a difference."

Vision takes guts. The bigger the goal, the bigger the gamble. But CEOs who don't take chances become failed CEOs. It's like a poker game. You build up chips in the game and you bet the chips back. In the end you want more chips then you had when you started.

Assess what the future wants and needs

That being the future customer, future employee, future stockholder, and the rest. "See things that may escape other people," says Maury Willman, CEO of Ergonomic Health Systems.

"I call the CEO's job 'connecting the dots.' That's your number one job. Keep involved in every level of your business and your market. Fifty percent of my time I'm in the field with customers, employees, salespeople. Every minute of every day I'm trying to stay current with technology. I contend that style and need for vision is directly related to how fast the industry you are in is moving," says Bill Coleman, CEO of BEA Systems.

You can't anticipate everything; you'll miss something despite your thoroughness. But with advance thinking you can cover lots of bases and react better when you do get surprised.

"The CEO needs to understand the market and the direction of the market and make sure he builds appropriate products to meet market demand. A CEO has a CFO for the financial areas and a VP of product development for actually getting the idea to market. He can hand that off to people. He can't hand off keeping his ear to the ground so he understands the nuances and can make reliable, secure decisions," says Nancy Albertini, CEO of Taylor-Winfield.

Do the hard work of research and assess by talking, reading, and looking

"Great CEOs understand that they need to really spend the time needed to get the vision thing right," says Jeff Cunningham, Chairman of iLIFE.com.

"Many years ago, I came to an associate with the solution to an issue with which we were grappling. She told me to go back and peel another layer off the onion. I dug deeper into the challenge and then, with a big smile of self-satisfaction on my face, went back to my colleague. Again, I was met with the suggestion to peel another layer off the onion…we made considerable progress because of my colleague's prodding and my willingness to step back, one more step, over and over," says Mark Miller, Group Executive Vice President, Right Management Consultants.

Talk to people about your ideas (a little)

But talk to them *more* about what's going on in their experiences. Everyone uses knowledge they acquired from others. Your own brainpower is important but so is the experience from others. Ask them: What are there core competencies? What are their dreams? How do they assess the future? Constantly gather bits and pieces of worthwhile information.

"I used to think I could do it all. I had to learn early that I can't do everything myself. The CEO needs more knowledge from more people than you can ever imagine," says Jim Perrella, CEO of Ingersoll-Rand. "And, of course, nearing retirement I'm more receptive to input now."

Your mentors come in handy here. "I check to see if there is an appetite for the idea inside before I go outside. I know where we are financially so we'll talk to bankers and consultants to get their thinking. There are a handful of people I will always call. Last week I called a guy and his secretary said, 'let me transfer you to him'. When he answered I could hear all this noise in the background so I asked where he was, 'I'm in the hospital, but I knew you were going to call and I wanted to talk to you,'" says Jerry Henry, CEO of John-Manville.

If you know of someone who might provide exceptional insight, but he or she isn't a mentor or you don't even know that person, get to know him or her. With a little tenacity, persuasiveness, and a cogent reason for a meeting, you can go in and talk with almost anyone you'd like to talk to. Nancy May, CEO of The Women's Global Business Alliance, says some of her friends are flabbergasted who she has gotten to meet, "I just pick up the phone and call someone I read about in *The Wall Street Journal* that I'd like to meet and I'd like to learn from."

"It's surprising how accessible people are, even the ones you think you could never get," says "Ask Annie" columnist, Anne Fisher, from *Fortune*.

Get out and about to a wider audience—globally. If you rely on insiders from your company or your expertise, you can get stuck in their own language, their own ceilings, and their own narrow thinking.

"I get stimulation from the world outside of banking. I love television news shows to keep a pulse on the community and the world. And I read and think," says Linda Childears, President of Young Americans Bank. "Then there are the visionary vehicles, the National Assembly that I chair. The heads of all social service organizations like the Red Cross, Campfire Girls, and Goodwill all participate. Those meetings cause my head to burst with so many ideas."

Look for relevant patterns in all conversations. Listen, and watch, then connect the dots. Clearly learn what others are doing and what you can learn from them. Second-guess their decisions to avoid making the same mistakes they've made. Then think about some directions for you to consider.

Go to the gurus

Get to some experts, especially in totally unrelated fields, and pump them for all the information you can. Get a 360° view. Look at the social, economic, technological, ecological, and political trends. The Pope does it. He brings in geophysicists and philosophers; people who have nothing to do with religion. He seeks to learn anything and everything he can.

Newt Gingrich was known for walking the shopping malls talking to ordinary citizens. In his job as Speaker of the House the citizens were the "experts."

Inside the organization the CEO also has to encourage the board of directors to contribute to vision—his "in-house experts." "The Board of Directors' role is to contribute expertise. They've had experiences with their own companies and they've likely made mistakes. Therefore, they offer qualified strategic thinking and principled reasoning," says Duane Pearsall, retired CEO of Columbine Venture Capital Fund.

Sometimes the best gurus are under your nose. Bob Haas, CEO of Levi Strauss, talked about a difficult time in 1984 where they had gone through all the fads and had become bureaucratic in their decision making. "So I did the unthinkable for me. I reached out to my colleagues in management and said, 'We're in this together. I don't have the answers. I'm not Lee Iacocca. I'm not the heroic leader. We've got to figure this out. Come back to me with your own prescription.' Lo and behold, being liberated from the old hierarchical model, they came back with what we needed to do."

Read divergently.

And prolifically. Read about finance if you aren't in finance. Read about the arts if you aren't in the arts. Subscribe to different magazines: *Science Today*, *The Economist*, and *American History* instead of only to *Fortune*, *Forbes*, *Time*, and *Business Week*. And don't just read today's issues; go back 10 or 20 years and read those issues. You can review research studies, corporate annual reports, industry association newsletters, and publications from the government. And most all of this is online to make it easier; you don't have to trudge to the college library.

"Be open from things from all directions otherwise you cut yourself off from possibilities. Have a sense of history. You can't know where you're going if you don't know where you've been. And a sense of geography too. Everyone on earth lives somewhere, comes from somewhere and therefore has different dynamics. You can see history and geography more clearly than the future," says Gary Hoover, CEO of Hoovers.com

You won't have time to read 15 trade journals a day, but you and your team can divide them up and go through them enough to stimulate each other's thinking. Clip and copy.

"There's nothing like reading and learning from other people. I remember when I was a researcher. I read biographies and business magazines. I adapted what they were doing to what I was doing. And you'd be surprised how much you can learn from sports too. You have to constantly learn and through the integration process you grow. It does require interest and desire though," says Bill Stavropoulos, CEO of The Dow Chemical Company.

Right now on your computer screen you can access *anything* at your fingertips: lists of companies and stocks and what they're doing; news clips from around the world through Bloomberg and Reuters; and current events, business news, world headlines. Today, you have the opportunity to read everything, study everything. But don't just read it, really think about everything you see.

But don't believe everything you read or hear. Jim McBride is the President of ATMO, Inc., a software broker in Moscow. "When I see CNN I cheer because of the misguided coverage they give of this country and therefore how it keeps my competition out."

Read:

♦ Systematically, thoughtfully, closely, analyzing every subject as you go along

♦ Contrary to your own thinking

♦ With constant application to your own situation

♦ But cast aside the worthless; save only the gems in your mind

Read history too. "The only thing new in the world is the history you don't know," wrote the late President Harry S. Truman. Surprisingly, a few CEOs told me for the first time they believe learning history offers little benefit because technology has made business so totally different than it's ever been so there is really nothing like it in history from which to learn. Of course others will say that what we're experiencing today is just what we had when the printing press was invented or when railroads reached across the country.

Look for what's missing

In all your conversations, reading, and thinking, ask questions to yourself (and others) like:

+ What is going on outside of my own industry?
+ What industry crosses over into mine or will in the future?
+ Who are the top three competitors in my industry?
+ Who are my noncustomers? (The ones you don't have and someone else does.)
+ What do they want?
+ Who is giving it to them?
+ Who influences this group?
+ How is disposable income being distributed in other places?
+ What analogies to my business exist and what is happening there?

It's surprising how an organized set of questions asked of several people highlights "what's missing."

The truth is that CEOs do talk to insiders and outsiders, like I suggested, but they frequently end up doing what they were thinking about doing before they talked to anyone anyway. Most go with gut feelings. One CEO told me about a group of eight CEOs he belongs to: They get together once a month. Each one comes with a current issue and it's discussed with the group. He told me that even if 90 percent of the group voiced an opinion not to do something, the CEO usually went ahead and did it anyway. If the CEO feels it's the way to go, or simply wants to go that way, he will despite counsel otherwise.

At least by talking to others, you've done some due diligence before you go and do what you wanted to anyway. Who knows, the more people who say it can't be done, the more motivation it might be to do it!

Again, look for what's missing. "Take the fast food industry who were traditionally only open for lunch and dinner. Herb Pertersen, who owns a local McDonald's franchise in California, came up with the idea of the Egg McMuffin. Overnight the fast food industry had an increase of 30 to 50 percent in their market. They went from two meals a day to three. Until the other companies caught on McDonalds had a significant advantage," says Peter Mackins, CPA of the Santa Barbara Visiting Nurses Association.

Come up with a clear direction

You have to think about vision every day—*to see around corners*. Short sentences. Short words. No buzzwords. One company tapes their meeting conversations and lets a sixth grader listen to it and describe what the meeting was about. If the sixth grader can't do it, the communication wasn't clear.

I've been told by some CEOs that they spend as much as 70 percent of their time envisioning the future. That sounds like a lot of time on "blue sky stuff." If you're focused: (1) you assess where you are and where you could be, (2) you assess the future and come up with some clear direction, and (3) you have the right things to think about every day.

"I'm *always* open and aware. I collect lots of sound bites. I eliminate the complexity and boil it down to what's really important," says Michael Jackson, Executive Director Field Support of General Motors Corp.

To develop intelligent foresight, you must work on it—at some level—every day, all day long and long before you become CEO. You must do this with every job you have, starting with your first one. "Every job I had, all the way through the company, I had a vision where I strived for my organization to be bigger and better. I took it upon myself in every job, from the beginning, to ask questions like: Where is the group going? How can I get the group where they should be? How can I get there myself? I had a lot of practice before I became CEO," says Bill Stavropoulos, CEO of The Dow Chemical Company.

"One of the things I have learned is that when there is a vacuum, it can be filled by anyone who is creative, has new ideas, and the courage to put ideas out there regardless of that person's level. What most often comes to mind is some ancient wisdom: Where there is no vision, the people perish," says Rick O'Donnell, Director, Governors Office of Policy and Initiatives State of Colorado.

A good CEO envisions and then paints a clear picture of where his or her organization can go. Clear, not complicated or ambiguous. "Bull sperm and guard rails. That's the expression we use at the company to remind us to keep things simple versus thinking such big visionary thoughts. Because the big money is in the simple stuff like bull sperm and guard rails," says Mike Moniz, CEO of VR.1.

Then live, sleep, and breathe it. Turn your "passionate point of view" into 10 to 25 words of action items. Wynn Willard, President of Planters Ltd., has his vision statement "Renew Planter snack leadership everywhere." When AOL and Time Warner announced their merger, the CEOs of both companies also announced that their vision was to "Win customers for life." The athletic shoe company, Nike, had a two-word version, "Crush Adidas."

It can be brief, just two words. Or it can be one sentence with five bullet points. The main thing is it has to be clear.

Share with the organization

You need to confirm and reconfirm that your vision meets their capability and their desire. If it doesn't, you won't get support.

You can be so close to the "forest for the trees" in creating your vision that you forget to point out the trees to the people who will assist in chopping them down. They will be the reason for success *if* loyal and dedicated. They will only be that *if* involved.

Today a unifying vision is more important than ever before. The amount of intrusive information in our lives is at an all-time high and multiplying every day. Life is ever more complex and the time to focus on any one subject is almost nonexistent.
— Mark Miller
Group Executive Vice President,
Right Management Consultants

You, as a leader, implement vision with the *help* of others. After all the work, questions, and introspection, you can feel that people know your vision, but they don't always. After you've done your vision homework well, pick a clear path and let people know it. Lock on and hold onto to it as you share it so it becomes the *common vision*, not just your vision. (Remember, it may have to change. We'll discuss that later in this chapter.) In the meantime, make sure you share it over and over and over again. First, to get support, and, second, to improve it with their "bottom up" perspective.

Allowing your organization to be involved in setting the vision is important. It changes the nature of the outcome. "In a start-up, one person might have a dream and share it with others as the business grows. In an established business, getting people to give an emotional commitment demands that you seek and use their input in shaping the future. Regardless of size, without the emotional commitment, a company is likely to survive but might not prosper," says Paul Schlossberg, CEO of D/FW Consulting.

Beyond coming up with the vision, the CEO has to get people to believe in and buy into the set direction. A Harvard professor described Lew Platt, former CEO of Hewlett-Packard, "He isn't a loud, extroverted guy, but he is constantly clarifying where he's taking this thing, and in his own quiet, blushing way getting his colleagues not only to understand but to agree it's right."

The common vision must be continually communicated because people can lose track very easily, and frankly, your vision is not as valuable as the common vision.

And communicate it with *how* people can make it come alive, *how* the organization needs to be constructed to fulfill the vision, and *how* each department or individual can impact the division.

"People want to reach their potential, be acknowledged, and feel they're making a contribution to something really important. The key to communicating a common vision lies in tapping those elements, then finding a way to express the sentiment of the company's vision as simply and directly as possible. The vision we've built in FMC I/T is known as 'CVP.' It stands for 'connected virtual profit' centers and everyone understands what that means and therefore is able to achieve it for customers, employees, and shareholders," says Craig Watson, VP of FMC.

"There is the *initial* vision and then there is the vision that's needed as you go along the dips and turns to the top of the mountain. The great CEOs see around corners. Some of it is gut instinct, some crafted after incredible research," says Russ Umphenaur, CEO of RTM. "Either way, when you have it, you need to involve your people for them to buy in."

At the point where George W. Bush felt his campaign turned to it's most assertive and assured position, he credited it to, "People are beginning to see my heart, they're beginning to see my vision."

With a common vision:

♦ One thousand people can work on separate but distinct issues.

♦ People tend to make more right than wrong decisions.

♦ And it can create the all-important company personality.

"Everyone working without a knowledge of vision is about as good as running in a race and not knowing where the finish line is. The problem I see in many organizations is that most senior managers and even the CEO know what the vision is, but nobody else does. How fair is that? After all, nonmanagement people are rewarded for the work they do in fulfilling vision. Maybe not as critically as the senior level managers, but still. So what if I told you your performance was not viewed as positively supporting the vision, yet you had no idea what the vision was? This happens in far too many organizations," says Helen Chacon, President, Common Ground Training.

Vision gives people a higher state to aspire to. It's difficult to go through difficult times, challenges, problems, conflicts, and anxiety *unless* there is a bigger, better goal in mind. People work better when they individually share a common vision in everything.

"Your people need a realistic and deep understanding of where you are going otherwise followers discover they are going around in circles," says Doug Conant, President, Nabisco Foods Group.

Vision takes time. One CEO said to me, "For 2 to 3 years I didn't get a vision. It just doesn't happen on a cocktail napkin. It takes dedication and passion." The fact is that sometimes it does come to you when doodling on the napkin but most of the time it doesn't. Either way, you then have to take it through the steps of sharing it to "test it" and change it as necessary for it to become the common vision.

It doesn't matter how or where you ultimately get your vision as long as you get it. Chanel's Karl Lagerfeld gets his creative thoughts in the bathtub.

Sol Trujillo, CEO of US West, got his personal vision early on. He has "aggressive vision...he is soft-spoken and even-tempered, but he has long harbored bold ideas," says *The Wall Street Journal*. One year out of business school, working for the old AT&T's operating company, Mountain Bell, he told his colleagues that he would run the company someday. "Even if you think that kind of thing you're not supposed to tell people," says Sol. "But I was always a maverick."

Many times people will think the visionary person is crazy. (Today, the crazy eccentric's been upgraded to visionary thinker!) Many times in recent history the person who was thought of as crazy ended up with a great piece of work and a lot of money.

"I always think outside the box. I always look at how *can* it be done versus *can't* be done. I can be a little dangerous. I need someone to rein me in occasionally without squelching my creativity," says Christine Nazarenus, CEO of e-catalyst, inc.

An executive friend was talking about his CEO to me, "He is so visionary I want to put a piece of duct tape across his mouth. He'll come up with 25 ideas a week! Actually two or three of them end up being pretty good. He has more moves ahead than anyone I've ever seen."

If the CEO is a visionary, he or she needs complimentary skills in the staff. For example, a visionary needs tactical doers around him or her. You cannot have visionary stacked upon visionary stacked upon visionary.

ONCE YOU HAVE THE VISION,
HOW DOES IT BECOME A "COMMON VISION"

By Larry Kopp, venture capitalist

This begins as early as developing the vision itself. The base idea must be exciting. People want to be part of making a difference. Having a chance to change an industry. To be recognized and rewarded also helps.

1. Start with small groups to evaluate the major elements. You can move faster in the data collection and drive evaluation stage with fewer involved. You can also combine more thoughts quickly, and assess complex patterns more easily with a small group. This group can be expanded on a temporary and selected basis for input assignments from critical areas of the company.

2. Make sure you have told everyone what you are doing top line and why. Have "experts" from important areas as contributors, and work to insure that critical management (especially opinion leaders) contribute and buy in. Polish the "draft" vision and its primary drivers, and effects on the company's revenues, costs, infrastructure and people with this smaller group. Communicate progress regularly, so that feedback begins coming early such that when the total product is shared, momentum is already built.

3. Share this draft with key leaders across the firm, and have them introduce the draft to their people both to critique and increase buy-in, as well as to determine the critical detail necessary to implement the plan. It is important to have done the homework preceding this exceedingly well, so that as the audience widens, the work product is viewed as solid, promising, and each person and department can see their role in delivering it.

Once you have the vision, how does it become a "common vision" *(continued)*

4. Realize that change, even good change comes hard, especially at first. However you present it, be sure the associates see that this effort has full support from the top of the company, and that it is supported by the opinion leaders as well.

5. To change means disruption (both to habits and personal territories). People need incentive to change. Often today, such as in the Internet or technology industries, the marketplace has trained us that change and speed of change is critical both to survival and to reaching the gold at the end of the rainbow. In other industries, this is not always so. People often would rather not change even if it means they will become richer. Change agents often find it easier, although perhaps less enjoyable, to change failing companies than currently successful ones (because there is no clear evidence for the need to change). In the first case, everyone is focused on survival; in the latter, everyone is satisfied with the way things are done now, for example, with the status quo.

6. Combine incentives to change in the direction of the vision. Include as many of the following as possible: A dramatic idea to change an industry, become number one, be the most innovative, etc. A dramatic reason to change—survival is at risk, but assured if we act now. A recognition and reward system for those taking part. And, gold at the end of the rainbow.

7. Realize that in some cases, outsiders may be necessary to train associates in the skills necessary to evaluate, analyze, and manage the key projects to a coordinated completion. And to help install the skills needed for perpetual change and learning.

8. Set up the change management group separately, but tied closely to people who manage the day to day. This allows the day to day to function, but to input to and appreciate the advantages they will gain when the changes are installed.

9. Take care of those that cannot handle change.

"It's fun to play around in the visionary role and not have to be responsible. It really takes a marriage of vision and strategy and tactics. Sometimes people are too caught up in the dream to see tactics. Or too focused on what's going to happen today and miss the next day. The right mix minimizes confusion for everyone. You need to go back and forth," says Bruce Swinsky, President of Kodak Imaging.

"You need vision plus action. Identify the target and the goal and follow-through," says Richard Gartrell, CFO of GoApply.com. "And through the hurdles too. Most people who made big change had ideas and had guts that carried them over the challenging times which are pretty much all of the time."

The great monkey wrench in everything is change

Change is necessary. And it will always be necessary, I guarantee it. "When I stand up before my people and say 'it's tough now but it's going to be tough for a couple of years,' I feel a lot of pressure regarding all the change. Last night, I was driving home and I was thinking about it and I found myself going 65 miles per hour in a 30-mile per hour zone. There was a car slowing down in front of me so I looked to my right and there was a tree; then I looked to my left and there was another car. So I checked that my seat belt was on and I hit the tree," says Leo Kiely, CEO of Coors Brewing Company.

+ Everything in this natural world goes through change.

+ To not constantly deal with change is to be foolish.

+ To be obstinate toward change is unproductive.

+ Change is a way to strive to perfect things.

◆ If things don't change for the better, they will change for the worse.

◆ Change can be painful but it offers hope.

Don't worry if your vision doesn't work out *for now*. Nothing works out like you thought anyway. The thing is to be flexible— and change *before it's too late*. You've got to be receptive to new circumstances. Besides, if your vision isn't "on target," you'll end up in the wrong place. So you might as well change while you still can. Almost every CEO has told me one of the keys to success is knowing when to change and get out of a potentially bad situation.

Change doesn't mean flitting from the latest fad to the latest fad looking for some magic mantra.

Change is not all huge steps. Sometimes it's little things.
Even relatively modest changes can be hard to accomplish.
— Ed Liddy
CEO, Allstate

"Today things are done in 4 to 1 time. Internet years are like dog years. The rule is to do four things to everyone else's one. Being right can be just being faster. You always have to try to stay away from the pack." says Mike Moniz, CEO of VR.1.

"CEOs often are forced to make un-educated decisions based on 'gut' feelings and tidbits of rumored information. The e-CEO cannot be firmly set in their opinions of process. What is valid today will be completely outdated and invalid next week. Constant adaptation and acceptance of change is an essential quality," says Brian McCune, Managing Partner of e-merging Technologies Group.

It's a fantasy if you think, for even a minute, that tomorrow will come to you in a tidy predictable manner. To *see around corners* is to sense the changes happening around you and relate those changes to your own and your company goals.

To enhance your own tolerance of change and even welcome it:

+ See change happening quickly.

+ Don't relax about it.

+ See cause-and-effect relationships.

+ See how it all affects your business.

Then:

+ Plan for the unexpected.

+ Reduce complex situations to something simpler.

+ Come up with some ideas to deal with things, for now.

+ Tell people what's going to happen, when, and why. Give signs.

+ Be the change maker so others have to react to it versus you having to react. (Practically put—eliminate your stuff before someone else does.)

Accept the fact:

+ Few people like to change involuntarily.

+ The price of change is leaving behind what you were comfortable with.

+ You have to take hold of some things and let others go.

+ You have to change from "what am I comfortable doing?" to "what can I achieve?"

+ And, finally, remember, change is eternal.

Embrace change that you see as inevitable. Don't be afraid or even hesitate. It's like professional bicycle racer, Mike Emanuele, says about fear, "If you fear crashing you'll ride timid and likely crash anyway." If you fear change, you'll likely crash so "jump out there where the limb cracks just to see how it feels to fall," as one CEO put it.

"You will have to break out of the comfort zone," says Alex Mandl, CEO of Teligent. "You have to have the stamina and courage with almost fool-hearted confidence for a pioneering approach." Educated nerve succeeds when dealing with change. You don't know what you'll get away with until you try.

And really, change is *not* a bad thing. Think about the technology that made your last surgery easier and resulted in a faster recovery for you. Think about the gadgets in your new car that make the trip safer and more pleasant. That's all due to change. If you really thought about how much better our lives have become because of change, you'd get down on your knees and ask God for more!

Most of us change out of necessity. Our desired goal isn't going to happen as a result of frustration or proactive decision; *we* have to change. It might just be the gut feeling that things aren't going to go right. If you sense it, but don't for sure know why, it isn't going to go right. Trust me. Change.

If the energy consumed to ward off the future from happening were channeled into *embracing it* and being the *change maker* everyone else has to react to, you might view it a whole lot differently. Maybe even like the Fireman Funds advertisement:

Life is a rush into the unknown. You can duck down and hope nothing hits you, or stand up tall as you can, show your teeth, and say dish it up baby, and don't be stingy with the jalapenos.

CHAPTER 3

MAKE DUST OR EAT DUST

♦ Strategic thinking.
♦ Decision making.
♦ Planning.

Man plans. God laughs.
Old Jewish saying.

Everyone has a plan until they get hit.
Mike Tyson, boxer

Strategic planning can be an enigma. It's a bit mystifying and it's probably the most challenging part of the CEO's ongoing responsibility.

Put *very* simply, strategic planning is looking, say, 3 to 5 years down the road, seeing what will be needed in all aspects of running the company, coming up with predictions to protect the company from undue risk, and then planning the corresponding tactics.

Of course, that's 5 years if you're a major company. For medium-sized companies, the horizon might be 1 year. For small companies, the horizon might be 30 days.

Meg Whitman, CEO of e-Bay says, "We reinvent ourselves every six months." Many "dot com" companies do it every 10 days! And one company CEO says he does it *every* day. (On the other end of the spectrum, you have the Japanese Internet CEO, Masayoshi Son, who has a 300-year—*yes, 300-year* plan.)

"Strategic planning is taking the major initiatives you need to put in place so you'll know where you're going to be at some point in time. That information then goes into the operating plan and that then goes into the individual executive's goals and objectives," says Bud Bilanich, CEO of The Organizational Effecgiveness Group. "It's was so well planned that I could always note the page and paragraph in the plan that my personal goals were tied to."

Regardless of your size or type of business, "Prior proper planning prevents piss poor performance," as one CEO put it.

Of course, there's the *other* expression, "plan your work and never work your plan."

Some CEOs say that strategic planning is an overused term, "something to keep you busy while waiting for reality to happen," that "90 percent of the strategic planning done is a waste of time," "the plan is really good at only *one* point in time" (meaning the moment it's finished), "seat of the pants is usually better," and "it's just an excuse for the company to pay for the team to get a couple of days at a golf resort." Now they didn't necessarily want to be quoted on those statements though!

*Important business success is about creating the future
instead of reacting to it. If you're reactive, you're already
number two.*

> — Stuart Blinder
> CEO, ITOCHU International

Good strategic planning provides:

♦ Direction with great clarity for now and into the future.

♦ Focus, thus avoiding the frustrating *non*focus.

♦ A point from which to make change; a "gut check" from which you can make course corrections.

♦ A longer-term view of things so people have a sense of where they are going.

♦ An opportunity to get to "the future."

♦ And, the potential of moving fast enough on the right issues with the right people. (If you take too long or trust the wrong people, all the planning will be for naught.)

To plan, you have to "decide" on things. Strategic planning evolves all around the CEO's decisions.

CEO DECISION MAKING

Strategic (and tactical) planning, as much as any of the CEO's actions, takes effective decision making. This is where you *make dust or eat dust.*

As the CEO, sometimes you know everything you can know. Sometimes you know only *some*, but not everything. And sometimes you know absolutely nothing—*but you still have to decide.*

The CEO is the drive and the ultimate decision maker who makes up the gap between "rhetoric and resolution."

"They say it's lonely at the top. What that really means is that it becomes so much more apparent that the decisions you make have an absolute bearing on whether the company will become a future winner or a loser. The more highly dynamic the market the more there is only one person who gets to drive and that's the CEO," says Bill Coleman, CEO of BEA Systems.

"I was the mayor of New York City for 12 years. I had a $28 billion budget. Each decision I made affected seven and a half million people. The stakes were high. I had to show confidence—in particular, confidence in my decision-making ability—because a lot of people had put their trust in me," says Ed Koch.

The CEO lives or gets fired based on the validity of his decisions.

> — Dave Powelson
> CEO, TRI-R Systems, Inc.

CEO decision making adds to that 1000 percent increased effectiveness. You have to:

* *Assign priorities.* All of the things that need to be decided on are not equal in importance. Like you do with time management, where you prioritize, rank the importance of the decisions you have to make. It's sort of like how one CEO described about putting his effort in the wrong direction, "you get to the top of the ladder and find the ladder was leaning against the wrong wall." Do not wobble or delay too long on committing to a direction. (No direction is a decision in itself—a decision to drift or relax and not move.) At least by setting priorities, you'll be going in a direction. If turns out to be the wrong direction, you can make a course correction.

* *Set a time frame.* There's a difference of opinion here from CEOs. Some say fast, not rushed, but fast is the way to go. First, to keep up with the fast-changing times and, second, if you do make a mistake, you have time to redo it. "Despite all the formulas, decision making boils down to the gut thing. And faster is better. Be 80 percent right and *first* rather then 100 percent correct and *last*," says Carol Ballock, Managing Director

Burson-Marsteller/Corporate Practice. Of course, fast can be relative: "I postpone a decision until I wake up one morning and know where my gut is going," says Deborah Triant, CEO of Check Point Software Technologies. The other thought is that slower (than you'd like) and methodical is the way to go. "Every time I take it slow and analyze the situation I generally come out better," says Robert Buhler, president and CEO of Open Pantry Food Marts. "It's easy and macho to do it fast, but it builds credibility when people feel you're thoughtful and reserved."

- *Gather and review up-to-date cold, hard facts.* Collect as many facts as possible, but not *too* many. Organize them. "You can wait and wait until it's perfect and you have all information possible, or you just have to go with your judgment," says Ed Liddy, CEO of Allstate.

- *Paint a scenario of the desired outcome.* What do you ideally want? If you haven't thought about it, how will you know if you get it?

- *Weigh plusses and minuses to getting there.* There will be trade-offs and compromises. Weigh the costs and the effects.

- *Explore the ramifications of all involved.* Who will be affected? "The CEO has to understand the impact decisions have on his people all the way back through the supply chain. 'Wear bifo-cals' so you see the close-up and the long-distance," says Bill Toler, President of Campbell Sales Company.

- *Go by the law, naturally!* A surprising number of people in or-ganizations do not concern themselves with this!

- *Keep human emotion out of it.* As much as possible, anyway.

* *Use your inner wisdom, have courage, go with your gut instinct, and decide.* General Colin Powell uses the formula $P = 40$ to 70, where P stands for the probability of success and the numbers indicate the percentage of information required. "Once the information is in the 40 to 70 range, go with your gut," says Powell. "Don't take action if you have only enough information to give you less than a 40 percent chance of being right, but don't wait until you have enough facts to be 100 percent sure, because by then it is almost always too late. Today, excessive delays in the name of information-gathering breeds 'analysis paralysis.' Procrastination in the name of reducing risk actually increases risk." If the analytical approach ends up different from your instinct, you really should stop and take the time to figure out *why* the difference exists. You'll probably end up going with instinct but at least the analytical approach was considered.

* *But don't broadcast your decision just yet.* If you, the CEO, make the decision public, you become its "sponsor," which can skew the support from the beginning. Better to have someone else come up with (the answer you wanted anyway) and let them "own it," sponsor it, and sell it.

Now, here, it does depend on the type of decision it is. How to execute some part of the strategic plan can be decided by the person implementing the plan, whereas in a crisis situation, everyone is looking to the CEO to decide.

With a decisive frame of mind, go for your strategic plan. But first: accept the fact that there are no "right" answers or directions. There is an enormous amount of information that you have to sort through to make the best possible decision. That takes a lot of work. Then you cross your fingers that some "luck" gets thrown in.

THE PHASES OF PLANNING

There are *47 different ways* to do strategic planning; what I'm laying out is *one* proven way that takes you through the "planning" as well as the ongoing strategic "thinking" needed in today's fast-changing economy. This approach can pretty much apply to all parts of professional *and* personal life.

> *Strategic planning is giving direction to people you serve. People need to know that there is a marriage of strategy and tactics. It makes them feel good about the company and where it's taking them. But good leaders simplify.*
> — Bruce Swinsky
> President of Kodak Imaging

In *phase I* of strategic planning bring in a bunch of outside experts on the future state of the world. Get different ages and different backgrounds if possible. Have them tell you everything *they* know as it applies to your business. Ask: where is the world going (for example, technology, regulatory policy, world events, natural events)? What are the trends and opportunities in the business world? What opportunities fit your skills and resources? (This is exactly what you did during the vision stage of talking to experts and otherwise reading, thinking, checking on your thinking, changing, and going forward.)

Peter Drucker says the goal of planning is to understand what might happen that would put you out of business and plan around that. So get the experts to tell you what might happen to cause that situation.

The "experts" might be some of your mentors. They could be paid experts. Or they could be your competitors. (The latter may not be as receptive to providing much information but you can learn it at industry meetings, through trade journals, etc.) The goal is for fresh thinking outside of your company.

With the ideas you get, plan the strategic planning session.

Those who are involved are assigned to come up with the top five or six most important issues in their areas and bring them to the meeting.

In *phase II,* go offsite, even if it's just across the street. Turn off the phones; put you feet up on the table. Get away from the tactical for now; go for lofty at this point. Get in a room with a white board, with knowledgeable people from your company, and have *free-range thinking* on everything you ever wanted to do better. Discuss issues, with the goal being to end up with the top five or six issues for the company.

The CEO is the driver of the strategic plan but he definitely is not solely responsible for coming up with it. He must lead an intense collaborative effort in strategic planning both from the top down *and* the bottom up.

The "top of the house" gets together and weighs how to manage, protect, and take care of resources. "We ponder the possible scenarios or problems that our company may encounter to reduce as much risk as possible," says Glenn McCall II, CEO of Global Venture Associates (and WildChild Enterprises).

The people in the trenches take the important issues and apply them to the real situation in which the company is operating. This level knows "what's happening" because they are closest to the different customers, different markets, different times, and different things going on in general. In the past you took the 5-year plan to the ranks; now they bring it to you.

With the key issues you can break into small groups consisting of people from all levels of the company. The "mix" in the teams ensures realism because they are the ones meeting with customers, testing assumptions, and exposing their thinking to other constituents. You'll get a lot better buy-in when you get to execution if you've included them in the planning.

The first-line people on up need to be encouraged to refute any ideas sent out from the top.

- *Set direction and scope.* The "mission, objectives, goals, resources" can be the outline of the day.

- *Discuss strengths and weaknesses* of the whole not just the parts. Ask "What strengths will we need? How do we shore up our weaknesses?" These questions re-establish your core competency so you plan around it. "We're not in the soup business. We're in the simple meal business. That's a broader perspective. It's like Black and Decker isn't in the drill business but in the making holes business. With that understanding of their core competency lasers can become part of their broader perspective," says Bill Toler, President of Campbell Sales Company.

- *Discuss where you are vulnerable.* What are the threats and opportunities? Like Peter Drucker writes, "what will put you out of business?"

- *Rethink the future customer.* Ask: Where are they headed? Who is the real competition? Now? Tomorrow? What competitive strengths do we have? Again, the front line on up should get to know the customer very well. Don't let this be "lip service." Really answer each one of these questions.

- *Isolate the various areas.* There are various areas you can influence to "move your business," *depending* on your business: product development, geography, culture, technology, production, facilities, distribution, real estate, advertising, promotion, publicity, investments, funding, marketing, and on and on. Here's where you discuss what participants brought in as their top five issues.

Consider issues as it relates to what the customer wants.

* *Plan your strategic end game.* Have a clear goal of where you're headed, how to get there, why and how you'll do it in both a practical and inspirational format. Sum it up so everyone "gets it."

We have a traditional plan and a bungee plan.
— Brian McCune
Managing Partners of e-merging technologies

The good about the practical approach is that it is doable and realistic, not just theoretical. "A strategic plan cannot create numbers that cannot be duplicated in real life," says Peter Mannetti, CEO of US West Wireless. "Your plan can state 'get to a billion dollars next year' but it's impractical because you can't hire 1000 people."

If it's just practical, you'll likely underachieve your goals. Aspirational plans go more for the "brass ring." Consider if you had all the resources in the world (think "pie in the sky"). What would you do? Go to the edge and then trim it back to center in brainstorming the possibilities.

All of these steps could be done by the CEO, or with his executive team, but including the people who end up doing the work and are also closest to the customer will make it ultimately more successful. The operators feel they "own it" and are "not stuck with it" when they are involved. Plus the CEO avoids the proclamation from the front-line people frequently heard in corporate America, "If those guys (that is, the executive circle) got any dumber!"

When you do finally decide, remember the "buck stops here"— with the CEO—regardless of where the idea originated. You sought their involvement but now you're responsible for the outcome.

Lots of sharing of knowledge and responsibility but the CEO ends up with responsibility of final direction.
— Jim Perrella
CEO, Ingersoll-Rand

In *phase III* execute the plan. Lay out the path you will take. Using all the convoluted thinking, talking, redefining, and "voluminous cascading plans," now's the time to turn your brilliant ideas into a fantastic, simple, succinct operating direction.

The "direction" must be something all conversations can include in its context. It must help people ground and translate complex systems and theories. It must ring true for general managers and truckers. And it must be relevant and ongoing.

"Any plan you do and leave on the shelf is an exercise, not a plan," says Paul Schlossberg, CEO of D/FW Consulting. "It should be short and be referred back to all the time."

It's important to remember that a plan doesn't make reaching objectives a *lot* easier but a little easier. In the real world it's like Bill Coleman, CEO of BEA Systems, says, "The CEO has to put the system in place and steer during the tornado."

Years ago, Gillette had a 5-year strategic plan to consolidate the European marketplace. While their executives were busily executing the plan, the Berlin Wall came down. One of the biggest events in modern history and Gillette was totally unprepared for it. So they missed the opportunity to expand into the Eastern block companies.

"Don't get so fixated on a strategic plan so you miss opportunities along the way," says Jack O'Brien, CEO of Allmerica Financial. Again, first-line involvement helps the top line stay close to the action.

To execute:

♦ Work to convert your strategic intent into meaningful work objectives and plans.

♦ Set specific targets and target dates.

♦ Corroborate your policies *with* your strategic intent.

+ Allocate resources you're going to need to meet your objectives.

+ Staff the organization to meet your strategic intent.

+ Clear accountability.

+ Set milestones to check if you're getting where you want to go. Allow time for the unexpected. Plan for "desperate moves."

+ Repeatedly prioritize, focus, and simplify.

+ Come up with new processes for formulation, implementation, and assessment of plan phases as needed.

+ Reinforce goals at every step.

When something goes wrong, it's back to *phase I*. It's a process that keeps repeating itself. When you get lost, go back to your plan.

(*Authors Note*: The preceding information was garnered from several interviews with various CEOs. And it should serve you well for solid strategic direction.)

Since this subject is so important, I wanted to provide a very detailed step-by-step approach taught at Vanderbilt University. Frederick Glossen, CEO of MB Industries, attended the program and shared the takeaway he had from it.

"I use the following outline to develop our strategic plan," says Glossen. "I've found that by forcing ourselves to go through this process, even at the moments you feel you can least afford the time or resources for something that doesn't yield a direct result, it is most needed. This process has a tendency to bring order to chaos, which tends to be the culture of most startups."

1. Prework one:

    a. Departmental/functional area input

        i.   Staff-level input on SWOTs (strengths weeknesses opportunities threats) and priority issues

b. Top team preparation: Individual
    i.   Assess strengths, weaknesses, opportunities, threats, priority issues, programs, and key result areas

c. Top team preparation: Assigned and circulated
    i.   Environmental analysis
    ii. Market and competitive analysis
    iii. Financial: history and forecast
    iv. Strategic and organizational diagnoses

2. Priority-setting meeting:
  a. Discussion
    i.   Environmental analysis
    ii. Market and competitive analysis
    iii. Financial: history and forecast
    iv. Strategic and organizational diagnoses

  b. Consensus
    i.   Strengths, weaknesses, opportunities, and threats
    ii. Priority issues
    iii. Strategic programs
    iv. Key result areas
    v.   Assignments for planning meeting
    vi. Core strategies

3. Prework two:
  a. Individual
    i.   Programs to address priority issues

  b. Assigned/circulated:
    i.   Draft direction statement
    ii. Draft objectives
    iii. Draft overall strategy statement
    iv. Balance resources

4. Strategic-planning meeting:

   a. Consensus on:

      i.   Direction statement

      ii. Objectives

      iii. Strategy

      iv. Key programs/action plans

      v.   Resource allocation

      vi   Communications

      vii. Review structure

5. Postmeeting work:

   a. Completion of action plans

   b. Coordination of programs

   c. Delegation of objectives/steps

   d. Final strategic plan

"To get the most out of your personnel I have found that you need to give them tools to extract the information," says Frederick Glossen, Jr. This can typically be done with the following questions.

Where are we now?

Situation analysis:

♦ What trends in the external environment, particularly in the marketplace, can help (opportunities) or hurt us (threats)?

♦ What markets should we focus on? What should our strategy be in each?

♦ What are our internal strengths and weaknesses?

♦ What are our core competencies that can be leveraged to beat competition, meet our customers' needs, and ensure our future?

◆ Taking our SWOTs into account, what are our priority strategic issues–those issues that must be resolved if we are to have an excellent future?

Where do we want to be?

Strategic direction:

◆ What is our fundamental purpose in life? Why do we exist?

◆ What is our vision for the future? What do we want to become?

◆ How do we define the scope of our future business, including markets, products, and services?

◆ What values will guide our actions toward our internal and external stakeholders?

◆ What are our objectives?

◆ What are the key areas in which we must get measurable results if we are to fulfill our vision?

◆ What are our specific objectives in these areas? When will we be able to measure results in each?

How we get there?

Strategies:

◆ What are our strategic alternatives—different ways we could structure, run, or dispose of the business?

◆ What are our selected "grand strategies" for the business, including growth posture and means of change such as internal growth or acquisitions?

◆ What are our external operations strategies—those things we will do to sustain a competitive advantage?

- What are our key internal strategies—those actions, investments, and processes critical to sustaining our external advantage?

- What are the handful of priority issues, or programs that will help us to implement our strategies?

Who must do what?

Delegated objectives and action plans:

- Have objectives and priority issue programs been delegated to the departments, teams, and people who must implement them?

- Have measurable and realistic action plans been developed to meet these objectives?

- Have we ensured that the plans and actions of key leverage individuals and departments are aligned with the corporate direction?

How are we doing?

Reviews:

- Do we have an effective top-team mechanism to review program action plans and progress toward objectives?

- Do we have a mechanism to ensure that lower-level plans, important to corporate strategy, are reviewed?

- Are individuals and teams held accountable for their plan results and rewarded or not rewarded accordingly?

What is important to recognize is that the plan is not static. Once the plan is in place, it is not intended to be put on the shelf and forgotten. Rather, the plan should be a living and breathing document that is reviewed quarterly (Quarterly Strategic Review Meetings and Quarterly Performance Reviews).

"The strategic planning process as we use it is to step outside the company and navigate it through the pitfalls if it is ever to realize it's potential.... It forces not only the CEO but also allows a forum to get buy in from the rest of the organization to shape and form the company," says Frederick Glossen, Jr., CEO of MB Industries.

WHEN THINGS DON'T GO ACCORDING TO PLAN...

"When it comes to the endless hours of strategic planning necessary in order to effectively compete in today's environment, there is still no guarantee as to what the collective outcome of these decisions will be," says Kyle Kundivich, Chief Strategist of Global Venture Associates.

"When plans go awry I first look at the plan's 'life-line' to establish exactly what milestones have already been covered, what are the new determinants and assumptions. Does the failure of this plan, at this stage, greatly affect the corporation or does it simply point to a new opportunity? And second, I ask how critical is the remainder of this plan to the company's longer-term growth and global scale? The important thing here is to avoid panic and to keep worry at bay. This is even more significant when you are the one that others will be looking to for guidance and motivation. I have found that panic can cloud judgment and worry stifle creativity, two of the major tools needed to overcome most obstacles," says Christian Boucaud, Country Manager–Brazil of S.M.J. Beverages.

Each planning misfortune is quickly analyzed to ascertain the major reasons for its incompletion. I ask:

♦ Was it due to economic changes that were outside of our immediate control?

♦ Was it due to wrong assumptions made at the very beginning?

• Was it due to our inefficiencies in any form?

The answers to these three questions help me to determine my next step. Do we go to 'Plan B' or is a whole new strategic outlook required," says Christian. "I concentrate on remaining calm, not allowing worry to fester in my mind, always remembering that 'worry is like a rocking chair—it keeps on going but gets me nowhere.'"

"You can get quite complicated in stragegic planning: checking the numbers, seeing where to make it grow, looking at the five year forecast, and running models," says Jerry Henry, CEO of John-Manville. "In reality nine out of ten decisions are made based on judgment, instinct, intuition, and taking your heart in your hand and going for it."

"My strategic plan is 'here's a cool idea, let's do it.' I seldom go to the board with really thought through steps. My mind compartmentalizes how to get there. I think about order. And I drop enough hints to the right people to build interest. Even getting them to think it's their idea. I go in with here's the idea, here's the steps, here's what it's going to cost," says one CEO.

Despite all these thoughts about your strategic planning, the truth is, as Bill Stavropoulos, CEO of the Dow Chemical Company says, "Strategy changes the moment you hit the battlefield. You have to implement then constantly adapt and change. So be realistic but also be optimistic."

CHAPTER 4

MAKE THE BIG PLAY

The CEO's role in operations is to:
- Delegate.
- Communicate.
- Plan for the mistakes.

---

*Don't let the desire to control everything get in the
way of doing what you're best at. Give up the ego
and let go, for your own good.*
> — Robert L. Johnson
> BET (Black Entertainment Television)

The CEO spends a lot of "fist on the chin" time with the "high
goals" of the corporate strategy: defining the metrics needed to be
looked at every day, making sure they are in place, questioning and
making decisions, building a process to avoid crisis, extrapolating
into the future, having a top team in place, providing resources to let
them do their work...*but* while doing all of this, the CEO can't then
get sucked into the nitty-gritty details of being operations.

You need to be above the fray enough to stay focused on the
vision and the grand plan, so you have to *effectively mobilize
your operations army* toward the goals through your delegation.

To make the big play, you delegate but *not* abdicate. You, the CEO, have a president, COO, or division heads for the "here-and-now" operations. That's their job. If your company is too small for that, decide which role you'd going to play: inventor, builder, or operator. You can't be all three. You have to delegate something to others—inside or outside.

People erroneously think the CEO has the *power* to run things. Not so. The people with the power are in operations. (And even more power is in the hands of the customer.) Operations make or break the visionary strategic plan because they *do* or *don't* execute. (One CEO admitted, "When we send dumb stuff down, fortunately, our front-line people are too smart to follow it.")

There is so little the CEO can—or should we say, could—do in operations, if good planning and good people are in place. "The CEO should be able to go for a month vacation and not make one phone call to the office. If he can't he's just a worker-bee, not a CEO," says Jack Falvey, CEO of Intermark. "But that doesn't mean he doesn't keep track of what's going on, keeping in touch even at the lowest level."

The CEO is paid to see the big picture. Again, that's *where you make the big play*. The CEO must be free from the "administration of little victories" (that is, moving the yellow file to the blue file) to focus on the bigger thing. The effective CEO knows the details in the big picture but just doesn't do them—which is different from getting his or her fingers dirty if necessary.

Operations is an area where you, as CEO, should honestly be able to say, "not much happens that I don't know," and still be able to take that "month vacation." How? That's part of the 1000 percent: the act of delegating.

Delegating is one of those areas where if you don't have the time to do it right, you don't have the time to do it over. If you've communicated the vision and the plan, people know where you're coming from and what you want from them. They become an extension of you in solving problems:

Choose what can be delegated

Here's where you take your vision and strategy and put it into short- and long-term direction *for others to do*. That means you have to release your control. The recommendation is that if someone else can do it, get someone else to do it.

Just remember, all strategy, all management, all processes, all systems, all decisions, and all efforts must serve the goals—either interim or end goals.

Select who will do the things that need to be done

When you delegate (so you don't abdicate), you always have to know certain key things in every job. You have to know what motivates people, in general, *in that job*. And you have to know what information or "intelligence" is required for the job, in other words, where the job might break down because there is an "information" breakdown. With that knowledge, you can delegate to the person/group who should be doing the job. As much as possible, match the project with the employee's skills and desires.

It's good to allow for some "stretch" that will help the employee to grow and develop in his or her delegation. If necessary, give some low-risk assignments to build confidence.

You obviously need to have competent people in the various categories you will be delegating: finance, engineering, research and development (R&D), distribution, marketing, etc.

Clearly explain their target goals as it fits into the grand plan

"Clarity jump-starts a successful result. I like to help people envision the end-state. The 'what' to be solved. Then leave the 'how' up to them. That way they own the execution," says Al Yasalonis, Nabisco Logistics Operations.

Frankly, the majority (that may not include you, of course) in society wants to be told what to do. Let them know what is expected as far as results and timing.

If a specific goal is superimportant and needs to be done *now*, tell them that. Give a clear directive but with some background, if possible, so they understand "what and why" it needs to be done. If the task is near impossible, do all you can to remove roadblocks so the person can achieve success.

Give a "due date" and treat them like you would like to be treated when given direction.

Let them do it

Expect them to be able to do it. They just might live up to your expectations. Wouldn't you when others expected it of you?

Trusting people helps them trust you *and* be motivated. Distrust demotivates. Only if your direct reports are motivated will they be able to enthusiastically inspire and instill trust in their direct reports so they can motivate, inspire, and instill trust in their direct reports and on down the line until everyone is committed to his or her responsibilities.

Even though you let people go and do the work that needs to be done, you still want them to know they aren't alone and abandoned. You don't get so "hands off" that when problems occur it's difficult to reengage with authenticity. "Make sure you don't abdicate your role in operations. The lack of operations focus looks like a lack of interest," says Peter Mannetti, CEO of US West Wireless. "When issues come up you can't provide input needed. It's sort of like the husband who's gone on business for six weeks then comes home and takes over telling his wife how to run the house."

You have to trust them to work well. The worst CEO says some version of "come back to me after you've tied your shoes;" that CEO is so involved in every detail that he or she really has no perspective and shows no trust in the people. If you're going to delegate, you can't micromanage to death and second-guess.

Now you must be aware when this isn't working, when the people under you aren't doing what they are supposed to be doing. So you need two guidelines upfront:

1. Have a process to "elevate" certain issues. One CEO wanted to know the top five customer's activities at all times. He wanted a monthly update on "where they are, where the company is with them, and where help is needed." Even though "delegated," those customers were elevated to the CEO on a regular basis.
2. Have an "exception reporting basis" where issues are brought to your attention that you weren't watching as closely but now need to be aware of.

Stay on top of things

Have periodic status reports (for longer projects). It's your responsibility to track what you've delegated. You can do it one on one or in a group. In a group you can go around the table, with each person updating the others.

You can stay on top of things and still give people a free rein. When you follow up, don't be all over the person. Have a certain amount of impatience but a certain amount of trust too.

A former CEO of Gillette used to invite himself on plant tours when visiting field employees or when customers were taking a tour. It was his way of walking around and listening to the floor people without stepping into his middle managers "territory." He could see first hand what was going on without appearing to be "checking up" on them.

Another CEO calls his telemarketing people and orders his own products. He engages them in conversation with, "what's the hottest selling item?" and "what problems have you had with this or that product?" and "where do you recommend I go for a product you don't have?"

Kikkoman Corporation's CEO Yuzaburo Mogi likes to visit supermarkets to see his company's soy sauce display. "I look at how the products are displayed. I watch the shoppers compare different brands. This is really the way to see what the market is like. You have to see it with your own eyes," says Mogi.

Like Bill Blount, CEO of Power Motive, says, "If the specific work is something important to your company, you better be involved."

(None of the previous examples means anything like one CEO who stood in the doorway and stopped everyone who was leaving to see if he or she had completed enough work to go home!)

When you see someone doing something particularly great, tell the person. Rudy Tauscher, GM of Trump International Hotel and Tower, says to the person, "You represent me and the property well. Thank you."

Although not delegating per se, I experienced this in Hong Kong and thought it was an interesting example of the "chief" staying on top of things: We were having dinner at the Peninsula Hotel. The waiter took our order, served it with the cowaiter, and the busboy brought clean silverware. But when it came time to remove dirty plates, the manager of the restaurant did it. I said to the manager, Andrew Tam, "In the United States the busboy picks up the dirty plates not the manager." He said, "I do it the opposite here. As I clean the table, I hear about the food and service from the customer. It's the time to learn if they were unhappy."

Have checks to measure progress

On a regular basis have a formal review that meets specific measurements, goals, or checkpoints. Find out if anything is falling into the "exception-reporting basis."

"It's like a football team driving down the field. It's several planned plays, not one," says Mark Pasqurella, CEO of Crown American Realty Trust. "My job is two things: the constant check on how we're moving towards our goal. And, checking where things are bogging down and I can be of help."

Keep control of resources

When people are busily *doing*, they aren't always paying attention to the big picture, especially the big "resources" picture, but you must. That's what you stay on top of when checking up on things. You exert control here; this can't be delegated.

Tauscher says, "When I talk to people and see what's going on I sometimes contradict myself. They have a budget but I tell them I'll bend, 'I'll find the purchase order to get something done.' I'd rather have 100 happy guests and one unhappy controller."

An executive who worked for Harvey Golub, CEO of American Express, told me the story of being in his office where he had two 4-inch-high piles of financials in front of him. He pointed to one sheet in the middle of one pile and said, "These numbers don't match." It was *one-tenth* off. But he noticed.

If you don't control the resources, how are you going to make money and stay in business?

Be able and willing to help (when asked)

Help solve problems, help with resources, help with timetables, or help with ideas. Demonstrate your ability and willingness to work in the trenches and get your hands in the mud. People need to know you know what it takes to make it all happen and are willing to do what's necessary.

One CEO told me he makes sure he does the simple act of putting on a nametag like the ones his workers wear when he is in the plant. It's a small gesture for them to see he does what is expected of them. Jeff Bezos, CEO of Amazon.com, is known to work on the assembly line when needed. Michael Eisner likes to test the latest Disney theme park ride. NewsCorps' Robert Murdoch "fiddles" with newspaper headlines. Jim Clark of Netscape would write code from 12 a.m. to 6 a.m.

"I can delegate real easily as long as I have confidence in my people. They just give me an update. I don't even get partly involved because then I end up with some ownership and that takes it away from the ones who are making it happen. Now, when my director of marketing has been out and will be for a few months and he asks me to develop a sales contest for him, I will. I participate when they want me to do certain things," says Dan Amos, CEO of AFLAC. "And I get involved when I don't like what I see is happening. For instance, when I got home the other day and was going through my mail I had a letter from our company, like all customers get. It was addressed to "Dear Mr. Daniel P. Amos." Now everyone knows that is not personalized. I told my people it should be "Dear Dan" or "Dear Mr. Amos." And it was signed "Policy Holder Service." Instead I told them I wanted the person's name. I just fine tune operations."

Plan for mistakes

Expect disappointment. You have to let people fail to let them learn. Despite your careful watch, with delegating, mistakes will happen. When you delegate, you give people the right to make mistakes. When they do make mistakes, you have to hold them accountable but without their job being jeopardized for it. Don't embarrass them. Do calm them down about it. Ease their fear of reprisal. (That fear is the biggest cause of more mistakes.)

"Delegate the authority to accomplish a task along with the responsibility," says Joan Gustofan, Vice President of 3M. That includes mistakes.

GE's Jack Welch tells the story of his first job in Pittsfield, Massachusetts, where he had a disaster and a plant blew up. He had to go to Connecticut to see his boss and explain what had happened. Instead of being irate, they were supportive and encouraging. "I clearly learned you have to make mistakes. Here I'd blown up a plant and I wasn't fired. I wasn't yelled at or even criticized."

When you delegate and "read back" on a periodic basis, take careful notice if someone is weak and needs to be "read back" on more often.

"I hate to make mistakes. When you start you make nickel mistakes, then dollar mistakes, then $10,000 ones. But it's still a mistake in evaluation, judgment, or execution. There is a high level I hold myself to and I hate to make mistakes," says John Krebbs, CEO of Parker Album Company. He's speaking for himself but my guess is he doesn't like them from his people either.

The CEO sets the example and hopefully inspires the people to follow. When an error occurs: admit it, tell what's being done to correct it, fix it, state how it will be avoided in the future, move on, and try not to let it happen again. That's if it's an "honest mistake."

Now, if it's to challenge your authority, you have a different problem than delegation.

The good news about mistakes is

• If you run lean, you can afford more or bigger mistakes.
• You usually mess up on something that you know the best, but you became lax.
• Mistakes are your best mentors because they are the sparks that ignite new endeavors.

One evening, a group was gathered at the CEOs home. They had just completed the building of a 240,000-square foot headquarters building, on time, and on budget, and this was a "thank you" celebration for the people involved. The CEO placed a $20 bill on the floor in the center of the group and said, "Tell us the mistakes made in this project and the best one gets the $20." With some natural hesitancy at first, people volunteered various "insignificant" blunders. But as the momentum built and people were seeing how the group was learning from the slip-ups, more and more were offered and people were actually having fun sharing their war stories. At the end, the CEO asked his wife, "Who do you think should get the $20 bill?" She answered, "They all get one." And they did.

The point of this story is that you learn from setbacks. By preparing for the inevitable, you create a culture ready, willing, and more likely able to react.

"Just think, right now, all over the world there are people exercising bad judgment. Somebody, right this minute, is probably making the mistake of his life," says comedian George Carlin.

Take responsibility for the outcome

When delegating: encourage, keep momentum, help solve problems, meet timetables, and stay within budget. Remain intimately familiar with operations Have reviews. Let operations people know you are there with them. And remember, *you are responsible for anything that your people do*. (That's for the good and the bad, by the way.)

Give employees credit for the work they do

Do the best you can to match the recognition with the project and the employee or team. Your intellectual capital is your most valuable. Nurture it.

You take the blame; give them the credit.

CEO COMMUNICATIONS

To delegate well: Plan. Evaluate. Anticipate. But don't "do it" yourself.

Since you aren't "doing it" yourself, you have to effectively communicate to get people to do it for you. That requires good communication when you delegate, check up, follow through, help recover from mistakes, and run the operations in general. It needs to be direct, open, matter of fact, appropriately humorous, and totally trusting.

Communication, and the lack of it, results in the biggest problems in the business world. You will be a more effective CEO because of this skill than because of all others. Communication is the desire but also the technique of tone and choice of word. It is the most powerful tool you have to do well or do harm.

The tongue is but three inches long, yet it can kill a man six feet high.
— Japanese proverb

"You can't overcommunicate," says Gary Lyons, CEO of Neurocrine Biosciences. "People need to know they can talk freely with you."

"Send me the 10 stupidest things we do," shouts Carly Fiorina, CEO of Hewlett-Packard, as she walks offstage at a company gathering. "I'll read it!"

That's pretty clear CEO communication. As opposed to the internal memo from a different CEO, "We know that communication is a problem but the company is not going to discuss it with employees!"

Communication is one of those areas where people do it all of the time and think they are pretty good at it, but others don't necessarily think so and the end result is a failure to communicate. The effective CEO can't let that happen on his or her watch.

"I value open communication," says Wynn Willard, President of Planters Ltd. "If it isn't there things clamp down and people can get secretive. The CEO has to go out of his way to communicate—up, down, and sideways. Everyone is entitled to raise their hand and say 'I need more.'"

A study by the National Association of Colleges and Employers concluded that the ability to communicate ranked first among personal qualities of college graduates sought by employers, and I can tell you for a fact that from the college graduate new hires to the grizzled old (or young) CEOs, that does *not* change.

Today, we communicate via voicemail, e-mail, letters, memos, web sites, video, audio files, printed documents, verbal conversations, and, of course, in meetings—department meetings, employee meetings, *new* employee meetings, and the rest. (*Note* that having all those meetings could be totally time consuming, albeit necessary so have some of them where everyone remains standing and keeps the meetings focused and short.)

According to a study by Pitney Bowes, workers send and receive, on average, 201 messages of all types in one day. That's a lot of exchanging of thoughts, messages, and information. (Some 562 million messages circulate via AOL each day.)

Effective CEO communication is *getting the right information to the right people at the right time.* There can't be any confusion between intention and perception.

"One button lets me connect to all 150 sites via voicemail to talk about the good things we or the industry is doing. I've found positive comments have to weigh 10 to 1. They also have to be and sound truly positive that's why I use voicemail attachments. I can attach the source of the 'positive' statement, say a supplier reporting good growth as a result of a store manager's effort, and simply enhance the message. Every person wants to have good comments circulated about them from the boss, tied to a genuine message from an outside source," says Robert Buhler, CEO and President of Open Pantry Food Marts. "But I'm a big believer in written memos, not e-mail alone. When put on paper, it translates into 'wow, I better get this done.'"

THE CEO IS ALSO CLO
(CHIEF LISTENING OFFICER)

CEO communication isn't just dispensing information but *hearing* it as well. You have to be the CLO too—chief listening officer. Everything in this book should remind you of that: listen to yourself and the person you want to be, listen to the world to find your vision, listen to the experts to shape your strategy, and listen to the people who execute your grand plan.

"I listen four times to the amount I speak," says Boston Celtics Coach, Rick Pitino.

Listen, long enough so people involved feel heard, then stop. Don't listen endlessly. "There is a time when they hand the baton

back to you and you have to stand up and lead," says Michael Trufant, CEO of G & M Marine Inc. "Like a doctor, you can't prescribe
until you diagnose."

To practice better listening, just remember:

+ Be *willing* to hear.

+ Be committed to learning and improving from what you hear.

+ Be open to differences of opinion.

+ Be courteous and respectful in your response.

"I'm the best listener I know. I'm the best listener in the company. I really listen. I get 80 percent of my information from
listening. A lot of people listen because they are afraid they'll
be attacked so they pay attention for self-protection. I don't worry
about that. I seldom even refute anything said. I just ask a bunch
of questions. How can you do your job if you can't listen and be
open to new information?" says Curt Carter, CEO of Gulbransen,
Inc. and America, Inc.

One female CEO who will remain anonymous had the most stel-
lar academic education I have ever seen. Advanced degrees from the
top Ivy League schools in the United States as well as the top
schools abroad. But she didn't listen. She was more concerned with
how she presented the right words than taking into account what
others were saying or how her words were affecting people.

When you are trying to listen, don't:

+ Try to read their mind; just absorb their words.

+ Be thinking of what you're going to say next.

+ Selectively absorb just the parts you want to take in.

+ Interrupt and derail.

- Give a positive response when it's really negative in your verbal or nonverbal reaction.

- Dream

"I listen to people. Divine what they are saying. Feed it back to them in an organized fashion," says Reuben Marks, Chairman, CEO and President of Colgate Palmolive Company. That's part of your job.

Listen. Then, say little, but be sure what you do say carries weight. The following guidelines will help you develop precise communication fast.

Keep it simple and structured

Strive for the "soul of compactness" when you speak. Think about the "sound bite" in the media business, where the interviewer extracts a statement that has impact and makes it the headline.

A McKinsey & Company consultant was telling me about a female client who works high up in the Clinton administration, "She listens with her eyes. A lot goes in and not that much goes out. She only lets you know what you need to know."

Brief isn't enough…

You have to have every word say the right thing

Author, Elmore Leonard, says, "I try to leave out the parts that people skip."

One CEO, who was known for being so brief, caused a little friendly internal competition. One vice president e-mailed to a colleague "hey I got a 'Nice job' from Joe today." The colleague responded, "Well I got a four-word complimentary message versus just those two words," whereupon a third chimed in, "Well I got five words today!"

"Each word seems to carry the burden of centuries. He weighs it heavily, considers it again, and reluctantly releases it to history," writes a *Washington Post* writer about Japanese Emperor Akihito.

American humorist Henry Wheeler Shaw wrote in 1850, "The more ideas a man has the fewer words he takes to express them. Wise men never talk to make time; they talk to save it."

Honestly, when was the last time you weighed every word carefully, reconsidered the words, and only then reluctantly released them to become history? You don't have to answer that out loud because I wouldn't want to either!

Frequently, people act like they are listening when they aren't at all. Don't let yourself get into that situation. Either listen or show that you are or get out of that conversation.

Some people are able to frequently "chat" you up only to consume your energy. That's wasted listening. You can extricate yourself from the situation with an honest comment, "We could talk all day about this but I believe I have the key issues so lets get on with making a decision."

Be like a courtroom judge. Listen to all sides. Reflect. Then be the last to speak. Not the first person to put out an opinion. There is a time to listen and a time to act.
— Michael Trufant
CEO, G & M Marine Inc.

Naturally, if you don't want others to waste your time, don't waste theirs. Get to the point. A company that distributes office supplies described itself in a press release with these words, "we are a leading supplier of nonproduction goods and services to corporations that value innovative procurement solutions." They distribute office supplies for gosh sakes.

A time not to be too brief is while answering a question from someone to which you've delegated. Say, for example, you could answer with a one-word answer but don't. Refrain. Explain a little more than you'd like. It increases people's comfort level when you provide more details. You never want to look like you duck out on tough questions or smooth over or move on with out dealing with important issues.

When using "few" words, you need to think about their impact first. Choose and use the right ones. When I listened to Leo Kiely, CEO of Coors, I learned how he frames things. Instead of saying, "What you should be asking me about..." he said, "Let me take you someplace differently." Instead of prefacing a comment with, "Let me explain this to you..." He said, "Let me paint a picture that might make sense to you."

To make the big play requires effective communication. Communication to delegate, to check on what was delegated, to correct mistakes, and to reward successes. It's preparation. It's sort of like the good shortstop who is waiting for the ball to be hit and is considering all the places the ball could go so when it's hit, he's already there.

Listen, first, and then give and take information:

Make communication two-way as much of the time as possible

Anticipate what's going on and engage in frequent dialogue. You get the best results by encouraging people to discuss the "opportunity, challenge, and what they think should be done" as you do too. It's a two-way street.

Now, you may be dealing with a problem and already have a solution in your mind. That's fine; a good CEO usually does. But you all importantly reinforce to the people that you value their opinion by asking them first and engaging in a two-way exchange about it.

Very often, it is easier and faster to delegate directly and specifically with no debate. But if you want motivated support, you had better not choose that approach too often.

Ask questions to clarify, verify, stay on track, track others, and avoid assuming

And to not look like a "know it all."

Answers to your questions direct you to the real questions you should be asking in order to end up with the outcome you want to achieve.

"Great leaders ask stimulating, provocative, and 'mind-bending' questions. Good questions indicate they are engaged, and they also enhance planning or decision making. You end up respecting their insights as well as appreciate their involvement," says Mindy Credi, Director of Executive Learning, PepsiCo.

"People used to come and talk to me and I thought they wanted a decision," says Jim Perrella, CEO of Ingersoll Rand. "It's not my job to give every decision. My job is to probe so they come up with their own decision. I'm a constant questioner."

Give people information based on how they need to receive it, not just on how you like to give it

Regardless of your best intentions, you will be misunderstood. Everyone perceives things differently. Do the best you can to consider the variety of ways others may take something you say or ask. Choose the best way possible to manage "what you send." Then listen to their response to evaluate how they took it. But don't assume you know. Ask how they interpreted what you said.

If you don't ask them, they won't ask their people and that will go down the chain, resulting in total mutual mystification. Even if you're *pretty sure* you know how they interpreted something, ask.

The effective CEO today has to be able to "play" to all audiences. That means personality types, cultures, and job functions.

When you do speak, be clear and concise

Don't talk with a stream of consciousness. Don't use fillers. Don't grandstand. Don't assume. Do speak up. Speak out. And speak clearly.

I had a car service in Los Angeles for a day of meetings so I was talking with the driver between stops. Although a few movies stars were sprinkled in, he mainly drove for CEOs. I asked when he observes them, which he can't help but do from the front seat, what is the more prevalent behavior he sees? "How few words they use," he said. "They are on the phone most of the time yet they have the other people doing the talking. And they don't seem rushed when they talk. They act like they have time."

Now, this was not a scientific survey but an observation from a man who spends 10 hours a day driving CEOs around the city. At the least, it's an interesting observation and from my experience interviewing CEOs, I'd say he's on target.

Never talk to someone as if you'll never again do business with that person

You know what I mean. It's the way you snap at the surveyor who calls at 7:00 p.m. or the secretary of the brokerage house who can't find your account or the clerk at the convenience store who lets other people cut in line before you without saying something. The ones you think you'll never see or have to deal with again. You may be right; you might not have to. But you may be wrong. The clerk may be the daughter of a client or your son's new girlfriend or someone going home to an abusive husband. Regardless, don't talk to them like you'll never see them again. That's a "gong" on the integrity bell.

You can be candid and not embarrass or berate. You'll get nowhere in the long run *or* short run by humiliating someone privately or publicly. Pay attention to your visual and verbal delivery. If your body language is like a neon sign flashing "you are *so* stupid," you may make your point, but you will obliterate your leadership.

Be tolerant of the fact that the other party is probably not following the same communication rules you are

Other people haven't had the upbringing, training, or exposure you have had. They may not have read this book!

It's important also to understand that when people disagree with you or object to something you have said, it is not dislike or disloyalty. It might just be their style. One result of good communication is that you are going to learn stuff that causes conflict. Don't hold a grudge over what was said.

Don't ignore how people react to you verbally and nonverbally

Don't guess; ask. See how things are perceived versus how you intended them to be.

Ask a version of, "How am I doing?" which was former New York Mayor Ed Koch's calling card.

Don't be tedious

For example, don't use the same listening response word over and over, for example, "yeah," "yeah," "yeah," or "okay," "okay," "okay." Give some variety, for example, "good point," "I see what you mean," "exactly," "that's right."

Nor can you have a look or tone in your voice like, "yeah, get on with it, I'm busy." Either response implies "I'm bored and uninterested."

Don't be a human loudspeaker

I can count on one hand the number of "loud" CEOs I've met. "Quiet power" is more the norm, with no "edge" in your voice as well.

My experience is that the less people think, the louder they talk.

Have a third-party review periodically

Pick someone to attend a meeting with you. Let that person be the eyes and ears of how you're doing. Most of us aren't that objective about ourselves when it comes to our communication effectiveness. Let that person know your goals and get feedback from his or her observations about how you're doing with others.

Take the time and effort to hand write notes to people

Receiving a handwritten note on good stationary from the CEO is a small joy to anyone. But write legibly enough so the person can read your note. The story goes that one newspaper editor's handwriting was so bad that one staff member he fired via a handwritten note was able to pass the note off as a letter of recommendation to land another job.

A well-written, handwritten piece offers many benefits:

+ It makes a more powerful point (throughout history the "pen is mightier than the sword" according to Napoleon).

+ It shows and takes deliberation.

+ It gives them something to read, review, and reflect on when needing a dose of appreciation.

When you leave a message on someone's voicemail

Leave your name and phone number first thing, before you tell your reason for calling so the receiver doesn't have to replay the entire message just to get it. Speak slowly, but make the message quick. Leave a sound bite or headline of why you're calling to avoid phone tag.

I had a CEO of a time management company call me three times without even telling me "why." I kept having to call her back and get her voice mail and ask, "what did she want." Talk about a waste of time, and that from an expert!

When everyone—including yourself—is swamped, overwhelmed, worried, distracted, or the mind is dulled from over work, it's all the more important to be doubly diligent with your communications.

CHAPTER 5

KEEP GOOD COMPANY

* What makes for good company.
* How to attract them.
* How to keep them.

He treats me like I'm somebody. He cares about me,
therefore I care about him. It's a definite privilege to
work here.

— Executive at The Frank Russell Company
about CEO, George Russell

Would your people say that about you?

The people in your company are the ones with whom you will achieve the results you are pursuing. It's never just you alone. You must attract and keep the good ones. (As smart as *you* are, they should be even smarter. I know that's tough to do but it's your job.) You need to understand people, mobilize, inspire, and maybe even shape them—both inside and outside the company.

The CEO job isn't a one-person show. You can't get it all done by yourself. You need to provide the vision and get people to buy into that vision to get them to do the necessary work. It takes lots of communication and visibility. That's where you have to perform. It's all about how you deal with people. You can demand and just *expect* them to do the work less than one percent of the time.

If people are going to want to work for you and with you, you have to be the type of person worth being around. That's why this book started with *be yourself, unless you're a jerk.*

You *keep good company* by valuing your employees more than you value your customers. Treat your people well and they'll treat others (like your customers) equally well. Treating them well doesn't mean being easy on them. Give people massive responsibility and they'll do it. Then brag about them all the time. Applaud and whistle too.

George Russell, mentioned earlier, and I were talking about hiring good people. He took out a pen, held it up in the air and drew an imaginary horizontal line. He said, "That's my level of intellectual competence right there. And if I hire people down here (drawing another imaginary line below his) what is going to happen to the organization? It's going down isn't it? If I hire people smarter than I am (drawing another line, this time above his head), where is it going to go? It's going to go up isn't it? You have to surround yourself with people better than you are—it only makes *you* look better and do your job easier.

GET GOOD PEOPLE—NO *GREAT* PEOPLE!

All CEOs tell me they surround themselves with the best people. Now you have to wonder, aren't all the good ones taken by now?

"Well, really it's more like you get good, average people that, with your guidance, become superior and go beyond their innate capabilities," says one CEO.

And another said, "Well the good ones may be taken *for now*. But it's my job to get them sometime."

As an executive recruiter, I provide career counsel to executives contemplating (or in the midst of) job changes. Most people reflect upon their prior work environments, so that they can define the "ideal" characteristics they seek. They consider industry and company size, but in short order, they spend a lot of time talking about the type of person they want to work for. As a general rule, I have found that people accept a new position because of their direct manager. They want to be managed by an individual who fits their self-image. The more common qualities they perceive, the stronger the initial bond becomes. There is euphoria in having identified an individual with whom they can establish a good working relationship.

— Katherine Cizynski
Senior Partner, Wiser Partner

Again, you have to be the type that good people want to work for.

Some say the biggest part of the CEO job is getting the right people. *You* are *responsible* for the outcome of whomever you hire. Regardless of the age or type of business, people "make it or break it"—and you. CEOs need to hire right, pay right, and be someone "they will walk over the edge" for.

Never pinch pennies on compensation. This removes money as a potential sore spot and preempts wanderlust.

— Christopher Day
Co-president, Packtion Corporation

Hiring right means getting people who have integrity, intelligence, judgment, loyalty, passion, intellectual honesty, energy, balance, drive, and vision in addition to being in the top quartile of the core competency required for the job.

*Hire smart people with good values who like to get
stuff done.*

— Mindy Credi
Director of Executive Learning, Pepsico

*There's lots of bright people in the world who want to do a
good job. Everyone is capable. You just need to find the
good match.*

— Steve Aldrich
President, QuickenInsurance

On average, you will have to change 60 percent of the people
who hold executive jobs during your tenure.

Finding the right people to do the work depends partially on
defining the work better. You have to have a clear picture of:

+ What is the work to be done?

+ How is it to be organized?

+ Who needs to do it?

"I look for a 'T-shaped' person like I learned as an intern at
McKinsey & Company. The person has broad knowledge in com-
puters, engineering, marketing, sales. They know enough to understand how each impacts the other. That's the top bar of the 'T.' Then
they also have a 'spike' of knowledge where they are experts. People need to be extremely capable in the area they are responsible
for— for you to confidently delegate," says Steve Aldrich, President
of QuickenInsurance.

To the "T," you can also look for the ones who:

+ Always seem to be invited to the meetings because people want
their input.

+ Are concerned and helpful toward what's going on in parts of
the company other than their own.

♦ Repeatedly help other people get what they want—their peers, subordinates, and bosses, too.

The recently retired CEO of Ingersoll Rand, Jim Perrella, built a career consistently practicing these three actions. "People help you become successful," Perrella says. "Doing it for peers is the toughest because of the inherent competition. But if you do it for them first, you'll get more support when you need it. An example was when one of my peers was working with our boss to make an acquisition. It wasn't my direct area but I helped him make it happen. I took the position of my peer and helped him sell his ideas to the boss.

Another example is when a colleague had holes he needed to fill in his management team. I gave him some of my good people. Not only did I help him but also, since they were good people, I got a reputation for developing good people. I came up through the controller route and that function traditionally helps others. But not always. In the beginning, by helping my peers, they did better than I did; then, when they were in better positions, it got turned around and they helped me."

GET THE REPUTATION FOR PUTTING TOGETHER A GOOD TEAM

"As the CEO you keep a finger on the pulse of the business. You have to be shrewd enough to know who to listen to and who is not helping. It is having eyes and ears out there observing for yourself and ultimately for the benefit of the business," says Paul Schlossberg, CEO of D/FW Consulting. "You get good people on your team, then you utilize them well."

After you've defined the work, character, action, and core competency required, then:

- *Spot undervalued, under appreciated people and give them what they need to bloom.* Clive Davis, former CEO of Arista Records was known to listen to songs on *Billboard's* chart. He was looking for bad songs that made it to the top. Then he'd find the promotion person behind that song and hire him or her. Other CEOs told me about interviewing some person for a job who had been credited with a success. Then search for that person's right hand and hire him or her instead.

- *Look for people who attract other good people by their own reputation and experience.* People are proud to work for people like that and that's important if you want to attract more of them.

- *Hire diversely.* When you "cross pollinate" different people who grew up in different ways, with different experiences, you end up with a mix that makes a good company.

- *Keep your commitments.* Make sure you live up to every one of your promises.

Smaller company CEOs have to surround themselves with great people but it doesn't take as many of them. Large companies need to grossly overhire and then weed out people to try to end up with the best.

How much time do you spend on people issues.
— Reporter to GE's Jack Welch

At least 50 percent of my time.
— Jack Welch
CEO, GE

Whether your organization is big or small, "Get honest passionate people. Someone with competitive drive, willing to succeed, willing to pay the price. Hiring is 50 percent, they have to want to be here. And 50 percent I want them here," says Bill Blount, CEO of Power Motive.

One CEO told me that his feelings toward every person he hires in his company is like getting married to that person. "We are going to be around each other a lot of time and there will be good and bad times. So careful consideration has to go with the match."

Now I don't want to paint an overly rosy picture here by implying that CEOs do things "right" most of the time. They, like you and I, *aspire* to be better. But even the best make mistakes—and people mistakes are the easiest to make.

"I'm pretty bad with people and not always a good judge of them. I've made a lot of people mad. I'm not Superman, I'm more like Popeye: 'I am what I am.' I don't try to be something else. It's back to integrity. Lots of people quit because they don't like working for me. But that's not all bad. That's why God made more than one company," says one CEO.

General Colin Powell says, "Being responsible sometimes means pissing people off." He explains, "Good leadership involves responsibility to the welfare of the group, which means that some people will get angry at your actions and decisions. It's inevitable—if you're honorable. Trying to get everyone to like you is a sign of mediocrity: You'll avoid the tough decisions, you'll avoid confronting the people who need to be confronted, and you'll avoid offering differential rewards based on differential performance because some people might get upset. Ironically, by procrastinating on the difficult choices, by trying not to get anyone mad, and by treating everyone equally 'nicely' regardless of their contributions, you'll simply ensure that the only people you'll wind up angering are the most creative and productive people in the organization."

Today, it's not just a matter of whom you want, but who wants you. "The best and brightest want work that is interesting, challenging, and empowering. The key to having work be interesting and challenging is to help people feel they are changing the world. That's what really matters to them. They want to look at themselves in the mirror with satisfaction. And they want to be able to talk to people at cocktail parties about things that are making a difference in the world. That empowers them," says Bill Coleman, CEO of BEA Systems.

Do all you can to *keep good company*: Find the best people you're able to surround yourself with. Constantly upgrade your "best" for other "best." Deal with whomever you currently have like they are the best; then motivate, inspire, and trust them. (They just might live up to your expectations.)

Hiring great people makes the person who hired *you* look like a genius for doing that. (And that's called job security because even CEOs need job security.)

To keep good people, you, the CEO, have to appreciate and recognize good action from your people. You also have to deal with the situation when they disappoint you. Through it all, you must protect them all the while keeping an attitude of good cheer about you.

PRAISE PEOPLE

Praise (or recognition) is a debt you owe to people making an effort and performing in an effective way. If you reinforce the actions that you want to see, you will likely get more of it. If you don't acknowledge them, they won't know your degree of satisfaction. Naturally, you praise what you admire the most, adding your reason for it.

On occasion, give your people a little more praise than is their due. Mark Twain wrote, "I can live for two months on a good compliment."

Recognize that people have different needs:

* Some look for security until they retire.
* Some want public recognition.
* Some want monetary rewards.
* Some want to be seen as expert.
* And, some just want quiet appreciation.

Pay attention to your direct reports and try to isolate each person's primary and secondary motivation. Don't give them what *you* like or need yourself. Give them what *they* need. Reputation has it that most CEOs aren't very good at praising people. More than one CEO admitted that he or she wasn't skilled at giving ongoing recognition. "I personally don't need it so I'm not very good at giving it," they profess. That's no reason not to give it to those who deserve it.

A pay raise is a one way a boss frequently thinks of as a way of providing recognition. But, as previously mentioned, people need to be appreciated in different ways. One female executive told me, "I was ready to quit because I wasn't receiving recognition. They just keep throwing more money at me. But that's not what I work for alone."

The following steps will help you, the CEO, to appreciate and praise people.

Be honest and be specific

If you can't clearly, succinctly describe the accomplishment, how will the person be able to repeat it?

Whatever you do, don't praise mediocrity. An ancient philosopher, Broadhurst, wrote, "Praise undeserved is satire in disguise."

Be short with it

You don't need a four-page memo, one sentence or even phrase will do it—"That was very clever." "Good job." "You were right." "Thank you." Is often enough.

"Note it" to others

Recognize the person's effort by sending a note to the individual's boss or in a group meeting or some other public dissemination.

"I send a note home so the spouse will see it," says Sue Canrich, Operations Training Consultant of F-O-R-T-U-N-E.

Lee Iacocca says, "When I praise somebody, I put it in writing. When I must criticize somebody, I do it orally." When anything is in writing it tends to be taken more seriously. It can be read several times or placed in some file for further reference.

Do it in a timely manner

" It's a great weakness of mine to not give it at the right time. But when I do people really appreciate it," says one CEO.

Just as you do it based on *how* the individual wants recognition, do it *when* the person needs it or will most appreciate it.

Before you leave the office, try to recall one bit of recognition that you gave someone that day. You just can't be too lazy about putting out the effort, nor can you be afraid to.

Give kudos in a variety of ways

Such as e-mail; sticky note on the person's desk; in the internal or electronic newsletter; with a gift or certificate for dinner, massage, or sporting event; take them or their department heads to lunch in their honor; pay for some child care or elder care; or provide consulting from financial services to office décor to home landscaping.

At one computer company, the employees get a self-stick company logo decal they can stick onto their computer. It's sort of like college football players stick decals on their helmets for touchdowns. Along with the decals comes a free meal or other certificates. At another organization, sometimes the boss hands out a "Payday" candy bar attached to paychecks.

"My Dad used to say it's only 15 inches between a pat on the back and a kick in the ass," says Bill Warren, CEO of National Inspection Services. "You have to do it well. One thing I did just today was when a newspaper reporter called to do an article about some new things our company is doing. I told him I would talk to him if he agreed to talk to several of my people also." Warren's appreciation of his people made them heroes at the office and at home when their quotes showed up in the paper.

Simply asking someone's opinion is praise. Knowing that the "top dog" thinks you have something important to say carries tremendous value to people.

Back it up

In other words, don't toss out praise like a candy wrapper. Say it and do something about it.

I'm writing to you in this book as if you were the CEO—and you are—of your life! But if you don't actually have the corporate CEO title yet, which is many of you, then pay special attention to plaudits upwards. Too often, people think that is inappropriate. That it's very misguided. Think about it; to work as hard as we know is necessary to become CEO, it's kind of nice to be recognized for it. CEOs tell me they don't need "praise" themselves. Don't believe them. Do it anyway. Be consistent—and be honest and sincere—in giving it up and down and sideways. Peter Drucker says you risk nothing by overrating your boss. If you haven't overrated him, then you have a powerful ally. If you have overrated him, get out.

CAREFUL ON THE CRITICISM

Just as you owe it to people to praise them, you owe it to them to critique as well.

I can guarantee you, people will disappoint you. Regardless of your great example, careful delegation, and optimistic blind hope, people will disappoint.

The number one rule is to not shoot the messenger when you learn about it. You can't punish the deliverer of bad news. He or she will clam up next time or sugar coat stuff and you'll end up not hearing about it at a time when you could possibly do something about it.

Before you find fault, double-check yourself: Are you responding to cronyism or favoritism? Are you looking at all sides? Do you have as many of the facts as possible? Are you being fair?

It's sort of like your parents taught you. If you're fair when you criticize, people know and understand. When you're fair, you can do what one CEO does, "I give criticism frequently. Get people used to it." Or when you're fair, you can do what another CEO does, "I seldom give criticism, but when I do, they know I mean it."

Criticism reminds me of the mafia dons in Godfather *movies who walk around in a meeting with a baseball bat and beat someone up. We don't carry bats but we all do it with words.*

— Russ Umphenour
CEO, RTM

The following steps will help you know when constructive criticism needs to occur.

Don't attack

Clearly state, "Next time, do this. Don't do this. Do this." Focus on how to do it right, what to avoid doing, and reinforce how to do it right again. Focus on improvement. Don't aggrandize or condescend.

Remember, you can cut like a butcher or a surgeon.

Give it in private—in general

Occasionally, a group approach works better but only if it doesn't isolate and embarrass. Look the person in the eye and explain. One executive told me when the situation is really serious, he literally switches chairs with the person being criticized. He puts the individual in his seat and asks, "How would you solve this problem? How do you think we should handle it?"

Boston University did a study that concluded the best way to deliver criticism was by e-mail because people were more comfortable giving bad news that way and were more likely to tell the truth. I don't like that approach. As long as you are courteous and respectful, you should have the courage to face someone, look him or her in the eye, and explain.

Avoid being repetitious or nagging

Don't use the words, "you always..." Or "you never..." Just be succinct and clear. As they say in boxing, "Don't throw punches in bunches." And instead of *stating* where or how they were wrong, ask to find out where or how they made that decision. "What caused you to...?" "I would have done it differently but why did you...?" "Are you satisfied with the outcome based on...?"

One CEO told me the story about a group of his staff that took to leaving at 4:45, then 4:30. I asked them about it as a group. They explained there was some highway construction and by leaving a little earlier, they greatly decreased their driving times. I said, "okay, I understand. Let's switch the hours from 8 to 5 to 7:30-4:30 till the construction is completed."

When you ask, remember the tone of voice mentioned in Chapter 4 on communication. It's very important to have no emotional overtone. Your message is simply, "You were wrong but I don't think you're stupid for it."

Be very specific and brief

Address the problem area, not their motives. Their action was wrong; they aren't bad people. People want to know when they were wrong. Wouldn't you? It's like an illness. If you know what you have, you can do something about it. If you don't know what you have, it's a lot scarier.

Ask them to give a specific, brief paraphrase of your comments to make sure there's no misunderstanding.

Explain the consequences of their action

After you talk about the action you want changed, let them know the consequences. It makes a bigger impression and demonstrates more objectivity.

"You may not have intended this…but this is the result of your action or this is how you caused people to be open to differences of opinion."

If you confront people with respect by giving clear and fearless communication, they just might listen and change.

They just might explain where you were wrong in some area that caused them to make a bad decision. And they may turn out to be right in their opinion. If you treat them with respect, they'll likely do the same for you.

Sandwich criticism by giving some praise, then convey the problem, then give them something good.
— Dan Amos
CEO, AFLAC

The goal is to set an example that constructive critique and feedback is the "breakfast of champions." In reality it is, but in the heat of the moment, it can look like a personal attack if not done well.

PROTECT YOUR INVESTMENT IN PEOPLE BY MINIMIZING THE NEGATIVE OFFICE POLITICS THEY HAVE TO DEAL WITH

Wherever you have people, you have personal interests and different understandings—therefore, office politics.

People do not wake up, blow dry their hair, drive into the office planning your downfall. They do wake up, blow dry their hair, drive into the office planning how to *protect themselves*. (It's human nature; if you don't feel anyone else is "trying to protect" you, you will definitely do it for yourself.)

"Self-interest alters acuity," says Rev. Forbes, Senior Minister, Riverside Cathedral. "The way you see it is the way you measure it and the way you measure it is the way you respond."

Minor differences of opinion can easily lead to major differences of conclusion. Minor similarities of opinion can easily lead to corroboration of conclusion. Add some accusation without confirmation in a "profit-and-loss" environment and you have office politics.

Everyone has the right to personal best interests but overall, for the long haul, what's best for all is the objective of the team.

"You can't get away from office politics, even board of directors have politics. To ignore it is both to be beholden to it and miss opportunities. If well managed it can ensure you are the leader. Every CEO has to be involved in politics if you view politics as communicating a situation to put it in it's best light," says Stuart Blinder, CFO of ITOCHU International.

"I don't believe you can protect people from office politics. That's what we're exposed to from cradle to grave. In our early childhood we had parents, grandparents, aunts, uncles, cousins, neighbors, etc. in our circle of influence. Once we reach grammar school we have teachers, classmates, and upper classmen. So it goes throughout our lives. Even in retirement we belong to different groups with different agendas.... In my company I try to encourage individuals with problems to take it back through the channels. But, I always listen to their particular problem so I know its makes its way to an individual who should be taking care of it. And we try to keep a fairly flat organization and that in itself eliminates an awful lot of politics," says Ron Brown, CEO of Maximation.

So, while on your watch, use the following suggestions.

Be open, honest, and direct in your communication at all times and at all levels

It's back to living your values and setting an example.

If there is a dispute between two people, call in both at the same time and say "Tell me what's happening here?" Don't let only one person have access to you. Don't let it fester. Bring the people together and resolve it right away.

At all times, whether regarding office politics or not, talk straight and direct—even if people dislike the answer, even if it's not politically correct. The effective CEO is considerate of, but not concerned with, being P.C. if it stands in the way of getting his or her message out.

Don't play favorites

For instance, share all information (as appropriate) equally. And when you're listening to their "side," consider that people don't tell the story the way it happened. They tell it the way they remember it.

Stamp out any "win/lose" game playing immediately when you see it

Don't engage in it yourself. Don't let it impact you. Don't let it blind you. Don't allow infighting and backstabbing.

A CEO who took responsibility about the office politics seriously sent out a memo. It stated that no more rumors would be allowed. "If a rumor gets to me I'll find the source of the rumor and I'll fire the person who started it. If I can't find the source I'll fire the person who told me the rumor."

In hindsight, he admitted it was a little harsh. But no one has forgotten it either!

Reward true accomplishments, not the "appearance" of accomplishment

Bad office politics can be about "show" and "spin." Don't let that influence you. Avoid having your people feel, "As if everything is controlled by a small elite group and you know none of the members to help you get in."

"The whole human race suffers from three basic misconceptions," says psychiatrist, Dr. Albert Ellis. "They believe they must do well; that other people must treat them kindly, nobly and do their bidding; and that conditions must be absolutely just so. These things are contrary to the facts of life. They are preferences." People think they deserve good fortune, good and easy times. It's frequently just good luck if you get that.

> *Take care of those who work for you and you'll float to great-ness on their achievements.*
> — H .S. M. Burns
> Quoted in *Forbes*

TO KEEP GOOD PEOPLE, BE OF GOOD CHEER AND GOOD HUMOR AROUND THEM

A good-natured demeanor is the Pepto-Bismol of business life.

How many sour people do you know who are successful? Go ahead, count them for me.

French essayist, Montaigne, wrote in 1562, "The highest wisdom is continual cheerfulness; such a state, like the region above the moon, is always clear and serene."

Good cheer does not mean "everything is blue sky beautiful." It's simply a conscious decision and choice about how you want to be— of good humor. As an example, Jerome Davis moved from General Manager to President of Maytag Commerical Products. We were talk-ing about the going on-board process and I asked, "What's been the most difficult part?" He chose to respond by changing the perspective and said, "Well, the most significant parts have been—" And he went on to tell some difficulties and challenges but with an attitude of good cheer enveloped around it in his tone of voice and choice of words.

Or it's like the memo I received from two different company pres-idents. The first one started out, "As you know we missed our bud-geted production sales by 7.21 percent and total production fell short of budget...due to wasted profits at...and improper quality checks...enclosed is your bonus for the period...."

The other company president (the successor to the previously mentioned president) sent a memo to the same people 1 year later, "Enclosed please find your bonus for…in the past our response was to penalize the entire plant and that was unfair…given the increasingly competitive market we are going to keep the customer happy by delivery…I'm proud to be a part of this team."

With a few exceptions, the two different presidents faced a similar situation at the same plant. The second one has set a measurably different tone and subsequent outcome based on an attitude of good cheer about the business.

Good cheer doesn't mean joking around. It means choosing a perspective that is positive and constructive versus destructive.

A good CEO recognizes the impact his or her behavior has on others and is sensitive to their moods. And the CEO has a genuine commitment to the well-being of others. He or she doesn't cavalierlike say some version of "take it or leave it," but takes the responsibility to make sure the intended message is the message sent. (When they do, they get a reaction like this one from a subordinate, "my CEO looks you in the eye…is warm, funny, charismatic, and friendly. Because she acts like she 'cares' I'd run through walls for her.")

The biggest strain of being a CEO is that you constantly have to think about others. You have to pay attention to your followers. And you have to be in a good mood, or at least act like you are.

Good cheer comes from the kind of person you are and from what you do outside your job. (This was discussed in Chapters 1 and 10.)

Don't take yourself too seriously—either the position you are in or who you are. Some people mix that up. When you walk down the hall and people see you, they are courteous for one of two reasons: either because of your position or because they know you and like you. You obviously want it to be the latter.

When you think about it, the vast majority of situations we encounter in business are not all that important to the big picture. In fact, only about 5 percent of the things that we get all wound up about are going to have any meaningful impact in our lives 5 years from now. So if you always strive to look at the "bright" and "light" side of things, it will, in general, serve you pretty well.

> *98 percent of the day I'm positive. The other 2 percent of the time I work on being positive.*
> — Rick Pitino, Coach
> Boston Celtics

We're the only species that knows we're going to die—you have to see that as funny!

The benefits of good cheer/good humor can be achieved though the following steps.

Reduces stress

It's true, he who laughs, lasts. There have been numerous studies about the physical benefits of laughing.

So you might last longer physically and also emotionally.

Diffuses a situation

It's a most effective tool to help people take a deep breath and go on. Unless you're talking about nuclear war, death, grief, destruction, chaos, or the world ending—find some way to use good cheer and humor.

One CEO told me about a pretty heated board meeting when one member lashed out, "You're such a moron." Whereupon the person taking the minutes spoke up, "Is that with one 'r' or two?" It was the perfect tension reliever.

Eases two-way communication with employees, customers, the community

Attorney Lawrence Land says, "I'm most comfortable just being me and that means using humor in everything. It breaks through the discomfort of talking with someone for the first time. I've gotten so much farther with humor than with regular conversation."

Makes work more fun

A great deal of time is spent at the office. It has to be rewarding and fun or people will just move on.

Comedienne Jonathan Winters says, "You have to keep fighting for a sense of humor because that's something they want to take from you."

Encourages similar good-natured behavior

The ripple effect of a leader's attitude is awesome. Don't you find yourself refreshed by cheerful people? Chiefs who whine and blame get that back from their people.

"Spare me the grim litany of the 'realist'; give me the unrealistic aspirations of the optimist any day," says General Colin Powell.

Have it in your consciousness, use it every day, and play with it every day. It's your duty.

Makes you strong

If you maintain this attitude, you will endure when others don't. You will achieve more and *more effectively* than a sullen person doing the same job at the same time. And you'll probably live longer which should make you even more cheerful!

Develops bonds sometimes even with the competition

After the $37 billion merger between Viacom and CBS, the CEO of Viacom, Sumner Redstone, explained how it happened, "He (CBS CEO, Melvin Karmazin) seduced us." People who are happy are a draw.

Today, you keep good people by recognizing their accomplishments, giving critique so they can grow more, protecting them from office politics time wasters and demotivators, all the while maintaining good cheer and humor.

"Admittedly, we work a lot harder at getting good people than keeping them. And that's a mistake because turnover makes it hard to develop a company culture since personalities are always changing," says one CEO. "I want people to know they are wanted for a long period of time. I've set financial rewards for the short and long run: retirement, 401K plans, monthly and yearly rewards. And it's not just financial reward. I'm old enough to mentor younger employees. And I make it clear 'we want you to stay, you're important to our future, and we want to be the first to know not the last to know, if we aren't treating you right,'" says John Krebbs, CEO, Parker Album Co.

To get good people you often have to entice them away from someplace else and to do that you have to be someone they want to work with and for. It takes a lot to get them to leave a good situation. Money is usually not enough. You compensate them competitively, rewarding them with special bonus or stock options when appropriate. Just as importantly, you work with them on their long-term goals. You help them grow professionally, personally, intellectually, and in responsibility. And, you follow through on commitments to them.

If you undervalue people, you'll lose them. You can have a great financial package, a challenging proposition, lots of opportunity for growth, but if people feel unappreciated, I guarantee, you'll lose them. First of all, they just won't take it; second, there is a ton of options for good ones; third, a lot of them have all the money they need so they do what they do for the passion and belief of adding value to the world.

One very sought after senior vice president told me, "I decided to leave because I was undervalued by two to three people. It was small things but important to me. My wife was sick last year and no one asked about her. We're in a merger and they want me to relocate but won't let me talk to my new boss prior to it, and one guy won't send a new organization chart reflecting me and my new role. It was a manipulative thing on his part. Now I'm leaving for another company whose CEO has demonstrated his care for the whole person and my current employer is scrambling to put together a package to keep me. But it's too late."

On a daily basis, each employee has to be treated like marketing departments are trying to treat customers. The trend is toward "customizing and personalizing" based on interests and needs. The CEO does that for his direct reports and his direct reports do it for theirs and on and on around and down the organization.

CHAPTER 6

BE THE NUMBER ONE FUND RAISER AND PROTECTOR

♦ The CEO's financial responsibility.

The report cards for CEOs are financial statements.
— Dave Powelson
CEO, TRI-R Systems

"Make the numbers" is the obvious advice. But making the numbers is just part of the CEO's job financially. You have the vision, planning, and execution part of running the show along with cash-flow, income, costs, and managing financial expectations of the public, your investors, and stockholders. Of all the parts of the CEO's job, finance is the area where you want the fewest surprises.

"People around you want to know that you're steering the ship on the right course. If you're providing surprises, you're sunk," says Chris Vargas, CEO of F-Secure.

There must be a means of knowing whether or not you are on course. The numbers and the analysis are the best methods available.

Finance is a complex and arcane subject. People get wrapped up in the numbers and forget about achieving the purpose. Yes, you have an obligation to be administrative and tactical to produce profit and foster that profit into capital appreciation. And to share, on a regular basis, that accrued capital with the people who produced it. And you need to do this over the long term.

No doubt, the CEO must understand finance; the top person can't be illiterate about it. But you rely on the functional experts—the CFO, or Treasurer, or Vice President of finance—to do the market valuation methodology appropriate to your company, multiple of earnings, free cashflow, multiples of book value, capital structure, equity instruments, etc.

As CEO, *you have to know how it comes in and how it goes out.* If you don't have a handle on the numbers, you don't have a hold on the business. Everything works back from the numbers. That's how you know what kind of "oil to put in the engine."

The financial reports

Understand the key indicators of your businesses profitability and liquidity—the company's balance sheet, income statement, and cashflow (including the footnotes). The details behind the numbers reflect the economic details of the business. By managing those details properly, you have the information that will enable you to determine if you are achieving the overall financial goals that have been established.

"The CEO looks at it from a satellite to catch the big stuff then zooms into the detail," says Michael Trufant, CEO of G & M Marine Inc.

Read the financial statements of competing organizations. Get a detailed comparison of their organizations as compared to yours. You can learn about the effectiveness of different strategies, success or failure of products and services, and see new opportunities. Plus see where they went wrong so you don't go there yourself.

"Ratio analysis is the key. It is the best means for analyzing companies of different sizes within the same industry. Also, if you are picking a company to compare yourself to, pick the best. Ratios are also very useful when comparing different years of a growing company. If industry standards are available, it's a good idea to see how your company compares against the industry norms. Industry standards are useful because they 'smooth' the effects of anomalies that may occur in just one or two cases. Remember, though, when you compare against the industry as a whole you are getting both the good companies and the bad," says Peter Mackins, CPA of Santa Barbara Visiting Nurses Association.

The CEO needs to know common sense areas like financial condition, accounting principles followed, controls put in place to protect assets, how money is not being wasted, and why things aren't overstated.

Measurements

These are indicators of your business' health. Identify the three to five most important components for your business, and develop some key ratios for measuring results. Boil it down to two to three key ones, like expense ratios or return on investments, versus a whole stable of them and look at them regularly.

Or have "less than 15 percent accounts receivable over 90 days" or "85 percent long-term, loyal customers" to measure and compare on a regular basis.

This is where comparisons of industry standards can be helpful.

It's important for the management team to see that "news is news" and that "bad news" must be dealt with routinely. Everyone involved must be encouraged to discuss the bad news and then take decisive and immediate action to correct it. Measurements are the "red flags" that are raised early and often.

Frequently, you can learn more from bad news or from things that did not go as planned than you can from being right. You might be right but not know why you are right.

"Good numbers or bad suggest how good the decision making has been in regard to assumptions," says Jeff Cunningham, Chairman of iLIFE.com. "If you have made good moves on assumptions, the numbers will reflect that. The CEO has to make those decisions and assumptions."

If you have a simple economic model that makes sense for your organization, and you understand it, you'll have a navigable tool. You don't need a lot of complicated measures because you can get bogged down by the minutiae and miss the big picture.

The source of revenue

You must understand the revenue sources and what the true costs associated with generating them are—which are fixed and which are variable. You should be able to do a cost/benefit analysis based on numbers. You should understand your company's profit margins so you can keep your eye on the ball(s) that produces income.

You will also want to know from where or whom your revenue is derived. Is it from one or two large customers, which is much riskier and gives you less autonomy, or is it from several customers who buy lesser amounts?

Have checks or measurements that constantly review what you can do more or less profitably. Consider the effect over the long term versus the short term. And always make sure more money comes in than goes out.

"Anytime anyone who reports to you fails, it's your failure. If you run out of money, it isn't the CFOs fault," says Curt Carter, CEO of Gulbransen, Inc. and America, Inc.

Expenses

Understand the expense side of the income statement and be confident that each is being managed effectively and with good timing.

There are always expenses you're responsible for but can't control. An example is Workers' Compensation. You can limit the risk but you'll never control it.

And there are the legal and tax implications also.

During analysis, you should segregate the costs which are not controllable from those which are controllable. You then have a truer idea of what you have to work with.

You do need to know the consequences of your action: the cost of what to do in a quick, responsive, flexible, and adaptive manner. And you need to know the cost of an exit strategy.

Growth potential

"I took this from a Wharton professor in a course I attended on value creation. I've preached it until I froth ever since," says Wynn Willard, President of Planters Ltd. "The best CEOs I know talk in these terms and they try to teach it because it isn't that hard and you'd sure like to have your organization help you.

"The purpose of business: more cash from customers to investors. The job of management: create value by facilitating that movement of cash. Create value by (1) increasing revenues, (2) decreasing expenses, (3) decreasing cost of capital. There is no other way."

Be able to evaluate new business opportunities, acquisitions, or partnerships. Have a general appreciation for depreciation, amortization, and tax impacts.

"You understand what is most important, and then you pray a lot," says one CEO.

THE AREAS WHERE ONLY THE CEO CAN ADD VALUE

With the financial indicators in hand, the CEO has to be able to interpret, analyze, make assumptions, set targets, and take action. You add value by your broad knowledge and experience. "Apple was loaded with financial wizards but was going nowhere. Jobs stepped back in with his knowledge and experience and the company has come back to life," says Hugh Sullivan, CPA.

The CEO adds value through his or her skills in planning, organizing, and controlling along with the "feel for the future" to help the finance people work accordingly.

The CEOs "feel" can extend to the tactical: the pricing structure of the product, level of overhead, determining which customers are good and which are a waste of company resources, vendor negotiations, etc.

Where the CEO really adds the most value is in the interpersonal skills, integrity, persuasion/negotiation, and leadership arenas. Today, people don't look at financial performance first; they look at who is running the place and in what manner.

Everything can't be reduced to numbers. There is the people side.
— Ed Liddy
CEO, Allstate

The CEO adds value with people and interpersonal skill. "I came up the financial route, at 29 they made me GM because they didn't want to give me title of President since I was so young. I could forecast and I could deal with plans to improve profitability. But financial training made me authoritative. When I became CEO I had to motivate people, become a nice guy, couldn't talk to others like I talked to finance people. That was never a part of being a CFO," says Dave Powelson, CEO of TRI-R Systems.

Integrity adds value. Some CEOs make decisions that are wrong for the business but right for his or her wallet. For instance, the stock prices are spiraling and the CEO opts to take the marbles and run. That's a demoralizing dilemma for the employees.

> *The captain goes down with the ship. Of course, it's with a golden parachute.*
> — Paul Schlossberg
> CEO, D/FW Consulting

The CEO's ability to influence adds value by the type of people that are drawn to his or her circle. For example, the law firm and accounting firm the CEO hires: What do they bring to the table in terms of their resources and contacts in addition to their expertise? It's easier to attract a great management team if they see good people already involved. Then, with a great management team, they attract more money. Surround yourself with good people, sell them on your vision, and let them do their jobs.

Even if you have a brilliant financial background, you need to let go when you're CEO. Don't depend on yourself, despite your technical brilliance. You have too many other things to do equally well.

THE TECHNICAL EXPERT(S)

You must identify the one person (or group) you can trust to give an accurate analysis of the financial results and strategy. The person must have outstanding technical skills so that financial statements accurately reflect the performance of the company. (The reflection of the results tells you "what." The analysis is more important because it tells you "why.") But that isn't sufficient; the person must also

* Be above reproach ethically; reek with integrity; be impeccable in character (just like you are).

* Be an effective two-way communicator.

* Be a confidant champion of the CEO's vision and be able to turn it into action.

* Have common sense.

* Have a temperament and personal chemistry that works with the senior team.

* Be someone you trust.

* It's a bonus if the person also is a strategic visionary.

* Has experience within the industry.

* Has experience with the types of activities your organization is going through such as raising capital or IPO.

* Is recognized as a reputable expert.

* Has a sense of urgency to get the right stuff done.

* Is able to deal with day-to-day operations, information technology, and human resources.

"But most of all you want someone who prudently manages finance and whose books are bulletproof," says Gary Lyons, CEO of Neurocrine Biosciences.

You want someone you can trust and not worry about the 100 things they are doing because you know they will be done in the manner you expect. One entrepreneurial CEO told me about his CFO who was doing a good job, "I have a great person running the place—better than me. So I've become chief check-cashing officer."

The basic job of the CFO is to be totally skeptical as they manage money, get money, and hoard money. No doubt, fiscal conservativeness is good for sustainability. Conservatism doesn't exactly fit the CEO profile we've discussed in this book. Although one told me, "there used to be three parts to my job: get money, be a cheerleader, and say 'no.' Now I'm devoted full time to saying 'why should I say yes'."

A CEO who is a visionary probably would need a CFO who is conservative. Conservatism is one of the Generally Accepted Accounting Principles and must be followed when presenting financial information. Essentially, it says when in doubt, take the course that understates revenue and overstates expenses.

In recent years the chairman of the Security and Exchange Commission (SEC), Arthur Levitt, has declared war on bad financial reporting practices of overstating revenue and understating expenses. That includes intentional misstatements in financial reports. What is currently called "managed earnings" was formerly called "cooked books" according to one U.S. Attorney, and practitioners are prime for criminal prosecution. And criminal prosecution means the CEO.

Fortune magazine listed a number of "CEOs as Felons" who've:

- Reported nonexistent revenues to make a losing company look like a profit maker.
- Concocted false invoices and revenues to meet earnings goals.
- Invented customers and sales to show profits when red ink was the reality.
- Fabricated inventory data, overstated income, and got PR firms to issue lies.
- Ran Ponzi scheme that defrauded investors of $450 million.
- Led staff to record sales for products not shipped—or even manufactured.

And these are companies whose names you'd recognize! Today, of course, their CEOs are serving time in federal prison or appealing sentences.

One CEO I interviewed told me about his early entrepreneurial days when he thought he'd cut corners and go without a CFO. He hired an office manager who proceeded to, among other things, not send in the payroll taxes. The IRS wasn't to happy with him, "I learned a valuable lesson: You can go to jail without the right advice. Today I have a CFO who is also a CPA. He's worked for a large corporation and had his own business. It's nice security."

PUBLIC OR PRIVATE COMPANIES

If you head a private company, you don't have to answer to as many people. Whereas if you're public, you do. Even if you're private, you still have to manage expectations with lenders and private partners. And they are usually closer, probably involved day to day and their reaction times to your decisions are faster.

In a public company the numbers and magnitude of investors can be vast. There's tremendous public scrutiny. You have the board, the shareholders, and the analysts and their predictions. Managing Wall Street is about managing what they will say. "Wall Street is statistic-crazed gurus with lots of specialized knowledge, desirous of glitz," says one CEO.

In a public company you need to deliver on expectations but you need a hot, hot, hot reputation too. One electric company manages from the balance sheet. They've done everything right financially. For 40 quarters there has been an improvement in net sales and return on investment. But Wall Street turned its back on them and the stock price has suffered. They are nothing exciting or fancy. They are an old line of business. The CEO continuously makes profit but he hasn't been able to "use" Wall Street to keep up his stock price.

Before we went public, we pretended like we were. It wasn't altering the company...it's just that we practiced living with the increased scrutiny in advance, for instance, closing books every quarter.

— Nimish Mehta
CEO, Impresse

"The CEO is the 'form,' the CFO the 'substance.' That is not meant as a dig on the CEO or a pat on the back of the CFO. It's just that the CFO is the reflection of the direction of the company. The CFO's image is a bit more practical," says Peter Mackins, CPA of Santa Barbara Nurses Association.

Investors are tuned to find the next "explosive" something like the e-businesses, most of which haven't had a single quarter of return on investment. As *Newsweek* reports, "If you cut costs, find new growth markets and please Wall Street, you will be richly rewarded. Miss your numbers, and your gone...CEOs who once counted their tenure in decades can now expect to hold their jobs for three or four years."

One CEO said, "you want a feeding frenzy, you want people afraid to be out of your deal."

Some CEOs say they spend up to 75 percent of their time with matters regarding Wall Street: talking to analysts, talking with big shareholders, managing expectations. (CEOs have to be concerned about the stock price because their compensation is typically tied to it.) The effective CEOs "underpromise and overperform" through *real* growth and *managing* expectations. (Which simply means explaining in advance to people *who care* what's going to happen to increase their confidence in you. You're basically explaining *your vision* to key players.)

Some CEOs *fear* Wall Street; some *use* Wall Street. It's much better to tell them how you're running the company than just reporting the number. And regarding the numbers, "If you're going to make "30," manage their expectations by saying "24." That is better than promising "30" and letting them expect "35."

Provide a positive earning surprise, never an unexpected negative. That's a sure way to generate a stock decrease.

Now you have the e-businesses that don't fit the classic profit and loss issues. Recent history has shown you don't need to make a profit to get a good stock rating. Sure, net business revenue is prized but profits are not factored in as heavily. They are, of course, nice but it is expected that in order to build a subscriber base, you need to spend enormous sums of money on advertising and retention vehicles. One company I've heard of purchases an item at $110 to resell it at $90. How are they ever going to get a return? (It's a company you see advertised so their investors think so.) Today, whether right or wrong, this is an example of a shared vision. It takes a different type of CEO and CFO to deal with the fact that they aren't showing a profit but their stock is spiraling up nonetheless. Of course, those companies can't go on forever without making money and just basing the value of the company on their stock.

"The most unenjoyable part of the job is being the CEO of a public company where you get graded and degraded all the time for optimizing the wrong things to make your company successful. The quarterly discipline is the least personally satisfying to have to justify. We did great last quarter. The company has gone from a half billion to nearly a billion. Every analyst says we're doing the right things. Our people were told they had the best earnings call ever and the CEO is doing a great job. Then in their report they said sell the stock and our stock went down four points. If I could take this private today I would and I'd double the gross rate," says one CEO I interviewed.

CHAPTER 7

ACT LIKE A CEO EVEN WHEN YOU DON'T FEEL LIKE IT

♦ Leadership on the inside.
♦ Leadership on the outside.

At all times, do what you think is right and eventually the world will catch up with you.

— Ernie Howell
Retired CEO, WPM
Packaging Systems

A good CEO is a leader, and as a leader, *you are always on.* You are *in front* and people see you—just like the military leaders of old riding white horses and dressed in flashy uniforms. You have to look and act like a leader all of the time, even when you don't feel like it. That takes mental strength, self-discipline, professional substance, self-confidence, self-esteem, and theatrics. Leadership is both inside and outside stuff.

Now, some say leadership is grossly overvalued because, "we aren't leading people into war here." All it takes to be a good leader is the same thing it takes to be a worthwhile human being. "A leader is just a moral person who is highly visible," says John Krebbs, CEO of Parker Album Company. "A successful human in an elevated position with a clear set of ideas and goals."

Krebbs is right.

Still, elevated means visible and visible means people are constantly looking at you for clues. You are never off stage. You hire bright people, and they see and sense when your shoulders are slumped or your teeth are clenched and you're stressed. Or they see a calm, confident, comfortable demeanor of straight posture and easy movements, someone saying, "things are under control." You set the tone throughout the organization by how you think and act— all of the time.

TO ACT LIKE A CEO *IS TO PERFORM—* BOTH IN ACTION AND ACTING

You have to give a *performance* also. Feels like the demands never ends, right?

Perform is a powerful word. In the case of CEOs, it means both their actions and their acting. In the CEO's *performance* is where we find the effort that makes up that 1000 percent extra: performance over time and performance at any point in time, including now. There is a Japanese saying, roughly translated: "A brief meeting lasts a lifetime." You and I want to make sure that in every one of our "brief meetings" we accomplish the action demanded of us.

"Leadership is a performance," says Carly Fiorina, CEO of Hewlett-Packard. "You have to be conscious about your behavior, because everyone else is."

"My goal is for my people to read me like a book by my behavior. As a CEO you don't have as much time to work into something. You have to get to the point and move on to the next issue," says Dan Amos, CEO of Aflac. "They can like it or not like it. Around me people don't have to go home and think about it. I create a pattern they can follow. If you were to ask my employees 75 percent would give you the same answer about me. Which doesn't mean I'm not unpredictable. That's part of the answer the 75 percent would give."

An executive who's experienced firsthand the career evolution of Craig Weatherup describes Craig as he's moved from division head to company president to Pepsi's CEO: "He's changed. He's been in the business for thirty years so he knows it and can speak about it. Today 90 percent of his job is building relationships. He's gotten good at all the chitchat stuff at cocktail parties where he shows a broad interest in people. He's spent an incredible amount of time with Wall Street and his style makes them feel comfortable as a leader. He's inspirational and down to earth. That's half the reason the company has such strong buy orders. Face to face his style is non-evaluative on the outside. Now you know he is evaluating you but he lets other people be his Darth Vadar. Craig's learned to stay above the frenzy."

Important note: Performing is *not* masquerading...but it is acting.

"People say, 'I wish I was as confident as you. I wish I was able to deal with adversity like you.' Behind the look I'm just crazy some of the time," says Brad Williams, President of Dakota Beverage.

Everyone *acts* on earth, all of the time. You act differently with a school chum, a boss, a competitor, a stranger, a friend. You behave differently when at a funeral, a wedding, at work, in a job interview, at the opera, or kayaking. Most people are wildly diverse creatures if you really look at their lives.

The more you're in the spotlight, the more you're required to act. Obviously, the CEO is in the spotlight. And CEO wannabees are in the spotlight too—or should be practicing for it. A smaller, less bright one but a spotlight nonetheless.

If you try out a variety of appropriate business behaviors now, you'll know what works in the myriad of situations you'll be faced with as CEO: the company spokesperson, chief advertiser, visionary leader, top salesperson, media expert, and financial guru.

Performing is taking the responsibility and enjoying the small control you can exert in life—in those brief meetings like the Japanese saying—by making sure the message you send is the message you intend in the brief amount of time allotted.

Accept the discomfort that frequently you have to "act" it before you're actually there. Now I'm not promoting the following example, but it was an interesting story. One CEO told me about his early days in the software world where a company's reputation was often built on the awards the company won. He had the idea of going into the company mailroom and pulling every copy of the technology magazine with a reader's poll on the best software. He filled out every card himself, figuring "we pay for the subscription we own the vote." They won that year's award. (Again, that it not advice proffered in this book. It's just an interesting story!)

Just as I wrote earlier, do not mistakenly think the daily execution of the 10 rules is for someone else closer to the CEO role than you. You have to act the part long before you get there. "If you act like it, and 'feel the part,' your chances dramatically increase of getting it," says Dennis Hoppe, President of Hoppe Management Concepts. "Clearly the traits that make a CEO must be evident long before the selection. Only those that exhibit these traits will end up on the 'short-list' anyway. So acting the part, without stepping on toes, and showing the emotional makeup necessary for those select few will get you on the list."

The late movie director, Stanley Kubrick, was described by an assistant, "He always acted as if he knew something you didn't know." And sometimes you need to also.

So whether you are a CEO, or already on the "list," or want to get onto the list, start incorporating the 10 actions described in this book into your personal and professional life.

HOW EFFECTIVE CEOs ACT—THE ACTIONS AND THE ACTING—IS THEIR JOB

In my time, I've been around some pretty good players, one of whom was described by *Business Week*:

"It was, as always, an extravagantly festive event. Some 500 guests of H.J. Heinz Chairman and CEO, Anthony J.F. O'Reilly, gathered under chandeliers in a mammoth white pavilion set up at the swanky Leopardstown horse-racing track outside Dublin....Arriving last to the pre-race luncheon, he and his wife, Chryss, stepped gingerly from a blue Bentley. As they made their entrance, O'Reilly began working the room, offering handshakes, jokes, and whispered asides with a politician's natural ease. 'When he walks into the marquee, the whole place comes alive,' recalls a recent guest. 'Short of a U.S. President's arrival, I've never seen anything like it.'

"Wherever he goes, whatever he does, 61-year-old Tony O'Reilly projects a commanding presence. A world-class salesman, bon vivant, and raconteur, O'Reilly has reigned as king of the $9.4 billion food powerhouse for the past 18 years. 'Tony is larger than life, and he knows it,' says Heinz director Donald R. Keough, a former Coca-Cola Co. president. In part, that's because he has performed."

The article goes on to report how O'Reilly became a Wall Street star and gave his shareholders "little to complain about." But notice the last few words, "because he has performed."

It is not to seek the limelight like some of you might cynically view O'Reilly's approach. And anyway, is it bad to be "larger than life"? Combined with arrogance, yes, it is bad. But if it is for the good of the company—the whole—the employees, the customers, the shareholders, the *cause*, than no, it is necessary to be "larger than life." Being "smaller then life" would be what's bad!

Good leaders should have good style and you learn that from other good leaders. Then you take the best that you've learned and add that to your own unique style. Voilá, you're adding to that 1000 percent.

When I met Tony, we were speakers at an insurance company conference in Cannes, France. We were both in the audience listening to the chairman's opening remarks. When Tony was announced, the biographical introduction listed his impressive business accomplishments both at Heinz and his own companies in Ireland. The introduction finished with, "…and now I'd like to introduce you to Dr. O'Reilly." (The audience applauded.)

Tony stood up in the middle of the audience and walked to the side aisle. He strode down the aisle and up the steps of the stage and went across the full length of the stage and got to the lectern. He silently looked at the audience with a relaxed smile reached inside his coat pocket, and pulled out a small deck of note cards. Again, he looked calmly across the audience as he reached into a different pocket to retrieve his reading glasses. He put them on. Then he spoke. I timed him; it was almost a full 3 minutes before he opened his mouth.

At dinner that evening, I asked him why he'd taken that route and that much time. (He could have come from the side like other speakers, gone up the steps closer to the lectern rather than all the way across the stage, and simply picked up the pace a little.)

He looked at me with his relaxed expression and said in his light Irish brogue, "Kill, or be killed." He knows you have a little less then a nanosecond to capture attention—to perform.

Now, I've told this story repeatedly and, of course, O'Reilly has done the same thing repeatedly. *Excellence is never an accident.*

Trust me, sometimes you will question your quest to become CEO: The days when you've repeated yourself 50 times because everyone has to "hear it" from the boss. The nights you have to attend one more function for some politician who has influence in your industry. The numerous times you have a meeting with someone from the media (who always misquotes you) or Wall Street (who just doesn't get your message) or the Board (whose expectations are unrealistic) or the politician, salesperson, vendor, and employee. And then you have the routine day…you arrive in Omaha, the tenth city this month. You check into the Holiday Inn, read the faxes, brush up on local events, and learn all you can about the people you're meeting, their names and their spouses. You have a chicken dinner, talk, shake lots of hands, and pass out praise and a company award. You go to bed with a migraine. And repeat it tomorrow.

And when you aren't on the road, you're up at 4:00 a.m., walk on the Stairmaster while watching *CNN*, get dressed, a car picks you up for the 2-hour commute to the office, sometimes a secretary is in the car to start the day's dictation. That pace continues all day and you get home at 8 or 9 p.m. at night. Most all of the weekend is spent on business phone calls. And then there are the pajama meetings at 3 a.m. for the Southeast Asian conference calls.

"Something intriguing to me is how often as the CEO I have to repeat myself. It's inefficient but necessary. A CEO has to repeat himself to a lot of people. People interpret things differently unless they hear it from the CEO directly otherwise it doesn't get heard in the same way. As highly paid as we are it sure is inefficient. It takes endurance. It becomes an athletic event," says Jack O'Brien, CEO of Allmerica Financial.

You can't relax. As CEO, you are always on and you can't show what you really feel. If you ignore this point, you are kidding yourself plus losing out on an opportunity.

Richard Marcinko of the Navy SEALS says, the two-word definition of leadership is "follow me." How you take the lead – on the inside and the outside—will set the tone and standard for your people to follow.

"The CEO has to lead the charge into battle with confidence, enthusiasm and the trust of his team. In a start-up company like ours things can get a little dicey. You are always close to zero-cash, you are facing 10-ton giants on competitive issues and you need to drive hard and fast straight at them. You cannot be afraid of fighting the giants and even if you are, you can't let the team see any fear," says Douglas Neal, CEO of Mobile Automation, Inc.

A different CEO says, "One of my people said he's learned to decipher my language. Every time I say 'no problem' it means 'oh shit' and everything's messed up."

As a parent, a politician, a police officer, a friend, and a leader—you can't always show what you feel. You choose the best behavior for the best outcome for the whole. And don't "tell your team how hard it is to be the CEO, trying to elicit sympathy from your team that you have so much work to do doesn't go over well," says Doug Neal, CEO of Mobile Automation.

This occurs in every walk of life, "Being in the NFL is like being in a car wreck every weekend, but you can't show it," says Bill Romanowski of the two-time World Champion Broncos. And Jake Plummer, NFL quarterback for the Cardinals, "I love it when a big guy hits me, gives out a grunt and I pop right up, look him in the eye and say 'is that all you got, big man'?"

"I never show my fatigue," says Las Vegas' oldest showgirl. (She's 38 in case you're wondering.) Her work is like riding a bull: looks good, feels bad.

Don't wait until you are a highly visible CEO to polish your theatrical ability. Work on it when you aren't in the spotlight so you can make mistakes that no one sees.

Leadership comes from the inside and is shown on the outside. Let's talk about the inside first.

I've accumulated the longest and all-encompassing list of leadership attributes gathered from my conversations with CEOs. You can use it as your personal checklist. Make a tick mark beside each point where you "recognize yourself." On the right, make a note of where you've demonstrated it lately. If you can't think of one, my guess is your people won't be able to.

AS A LEADER, YOU:

+ Use vision to motivate others. (*Note*: Your example goes here.)
+ Provide clear direction, communicate priorities, and define expectations.
+ Are proactive, step forward, and take risks.
+ Inspire others to be self-starting leaders themselves.
+ Drive others toward growth while growing yourself.
+ Recognize and reward others' growth too.

- Stand up for your people and don't ever leave them hanging out on a limb.

- Take on the fight to defend them if necessary.

- Look outward for ideas all of the time with a real curiosity of how to create value.

- Are a role model and set an example, particularly an example of integrity.

- Support, mentor, and listen.

- Walk the talk.

- Relay and relate information in a manner which is understood to individuals with varying responsibility/authority.

- Delegate and mobilize a diverse group while observing all players to analyze their contribution.

- Meet commitments and get others to also.

- Are flexible, adapt, and deal with change.

- Handle confrontational situations without being emotional.

- Think on your feet when presented with questions and situations.

- Seek input, allow people to "pressure up" concerns and issues (a form of reverse delegation), and encourage reflective back talk and even dissent.

- Create (or reshape) a culture or a corporate point of view.

- Gets consensus sometimes and doesn't at other times.

- Are visible—have a style that supports substance and has a personal impact.

- Protect people and collaborate; if you mess up, you're doing it right; embrace error; drive out fear.

+ Are successful and show others how to be.

+ Are fair and respect others (have the integrity piece) no matter how bad a situation you may be in.

+ Make hard decisions, are imaginative, and solve problems.

+ Admit when you are wrong.

+ Get things done that make a difference.

+ Are selfless in terms of acknowledging others' contributions.

+ Encourage innovation and remove barriers.

+ Are intuitive.

+ Take risks.

+ Provide proper feedback.

+ Know the world owes you nothing.

Sounds like a list of what a good person does *just as part of living*. It is *not* behavior reserved for a person entrusted with authority, with a title of CEO, or the role of leader. It's a behavior list for *you and I* to aspire to every day. It's that 1000 percent extra needed.

Every action on the list you do not have dictates how quickly the end will approach.

Note: Take a moment to think back at people you've seen in a position of power who haven't done many of the things on the list. Make a personal commitment not to be like that person. Or else you'll be remembered, like him or her, for the wrong thing. That is not the legacy you want to have.

"You can acquire leadership. You have to start early and get good exposure because you build on it by watching others. It's partly innate and partly acquired," says Lee Roberts, CEO of FileNET.

"The world is a big place. Seek to make a difference in the short time that you may have on the planet," says Thome Matisz, CEO of Solotec. "Your ashes are all equal in the end except the legacy is different."

When I stepped down as CEO I sent an email to all my employees to let them know what I was doing. I received 300 replies, everyone saying something positive about my leadership. It was the most rewarding thing in my life.
— Sam Ginn
Chairman, Vodafone Airtouch

Now let's look at the outside stuff....

Sorry, how you act and appear does matter.

CEO THEATRICS

If not to the CEO, the company leader, who are people going to look to? Of course, it has to be you. And when they look up, they want to see someone in control of his or her space, in command of his or her facilities. They also want consistency. You can't be "up" one day and "down" the next. Which doesn't mean you can't bring some surprise into the picture. That can be part of your consistency—unpredictability.

"People read me like a book. When I get off the elevator people are looking at me to see how I'm feeling. If I'm having a problem with the Board and it's getting ugly, I'm not going to show it. It's the part of my job I can only talk about at home with my wife. I didn't anticipate the energy level it takes due to the acting," says Jerry Henry, CEO of John-Manville. "When you feel bad, you act like you feel good. When you're upset, you cover it. When you're not upset you might have to act upset. If you're really disappointed you can't show it. What else do you call that but acting?"

As CEO, your shining moment is *all of the time*. Life is theater and the CEO has to be prepared to take center stage. Come Friday, you'll be exhausted, but you'll feel satisfied that you gave people the show you wanted them to see. (Remember, "show" is not artifice. It's the responsibility to affect people the way you need to.)

Again, don't wait until you're CEO to embrace theatrics. If you don't pay much attention to this today, tomorrow you'll end up light years behind someone else who does.

"My actions affect everybody else. If I let the tension get to me, the tension ends up running high with everyone else," says Linda Childears, CEO of Young Americans Bank.

"Good CEOs do not allow themselves to act threatened and not combative. In almost every way they act even when they say they don't," says Dinita Johnson Hughes, CEO of Edgewater System for Balanced Living.

And you may have to *act* your acting until you *own* your acting. "I've always believed in 'fake it till you make it,'" says Mike Wilfley, CEO of Wilfley & Sons. "It's not so much how you act but how you project. I recently got appointed to the chair of the Denver Museum of Natural History. I have to think about how to present on this larger stage now. I can work with the cowboys in the field and the engineers in the plant and the country club set but now I also have to work with the mayor and those types."

One department head was described by a subordinate: "He's off the chart emotionally and physically. He gets agitated, tapping his foot, fidgeting with his pen, twisting his facial expressions. It makes me uneasy and I have to question if he acts the way he thinks." That person will not make it to CEO; I guarantee it. He or she may be brilliant, but without the look we expect from a leader, he won't get followership. It's not fair; it's just reality.

There was a time people used to think I was so standoffish. I didn't realize how I came across and that hurt me. So I have to make myself act available and friendly.

— Monique Robittaile
CEO, Brouliette & Sons

CEO "Ed" is very conservative, meticulous in dress, proper, even a little suburban looking—you know dignified and reserved. He was opening a new location of his retail stores and he let the local business newspaper photographer talk him into "shoeless, jumping on a bed with glee" for a photo. That's the shot that made the cover of the business section. "In six seconds I changed my whole image," he says. "People tell me I'm creative, more casual, fun, and 'with it' now. And it's all due to that little bit of acting on my part."

Five minutes of the "right" (or the "wrong") action can be worth 5 months or years of hard work.

You need to be able to "turn it on," but it's just as important to know when to turn it off sometimes. "Too much intimidation can get people to shut up before they start talking, and impedes relationship," says Brian McCune, Managing Partner of e-merging technologies group.

Make sure someone else is the center of attention as needed. "When I'm traveling around the country visiting my people I give eye contact to the leader of the meeting continuously. Everyone's looking at me but I look at the person talking or who should be talking, the local leader. I want the rest to pay attention to whoever's talking not just to me," says Steve Aldrich, CEO of QuickenInsurance.

In most situations you generally need to appear cool, calm, collected, confident, competent, and comfortable. Really, what else can you do and have any hope that people will follow you? To accomplish this, you need to follow these steps.

Slow down

Yes, in an age of quick, quick, quick, slow down. Not your thinking or action but your movement, walking, talking, and gesticulating. And no, not in a boring, tired, loser way, but purposefully paced.

Power is characteristically calm. Weak is characteristically harried and distracted.

When John McCain accepted the New Hampshire primary win, he practiced his speech for 3 hours, reminding himself, "be slow, slow, slow."

Some of the CEOs I've talked with have unbelievable wealth. Money has bought them freedom. Well your physical demeanor buys you freedom too. You don't have to "run around the track for anybody." Slowing down shows that.

(Can you believe this? There is a drug popularized in Hollywood called Botox. It was launched 10 years ago to help patients with severe eye spasms. But some people are using it—at $500 per injection—to look calm, more unruffled in their demeanor, and unshakable in their composure.)

"Leaders do not appear to be rushed even if time is critical," says Markus Schweig, Vice President of Microsoft. They take the time to do it and don't hurry through it.

You can have an at-ease looseness based on total physical control when you move slower. It comes across as low key but forceful, respectful but comfortable.

Move purposefully and let the audience take in everything (because I guarantee you that they are). Just think how the Queen of England walks into a room versus Tony Blair. Which one looks like he or she has to prove something?

There is a high degree of risk in the CEO job and people look for more confidence from you.

Now all of this doesn't mean you cut down on energy. People need to see you can generate excitement with your presence and calm charisma.

Stand up tall and straight

Yes, like your Mother told you—good old scapular retraction (the scientific word for it).

I don't care how tall you are; hold yourself to your full height. It makes you look more energetic, taller, thinner, and improves your voice. Now, should any of that matter being a leader? No. But in reality, does it? Yes.

"Hunched" looks scared, tired, and defeated. "Straight" looks confident, competent, and comfortable. So right now, lift the rib cage off the pelvis—and keep it that way until you die.

I pretend I'm always being viedeotaped.
— Quin Tran
VP and GM Worldwide, Xerox Colorgraphic.

Carolyn Creager, CEO of Executive Physical Therapy Inc., trains CEOs. "Sometimes I find those who feel it's beneath them to take care of their health. But that affects their energy, their posture, their look of an "ability to deliver. A weak physical demeanor carries over into their substance or at least delivery of substance."

Control your hands

People believe your fingers. (Please, I know what you're thinking, so don't go there, okay?) People *listen* to your fingers.

Clenched fists, drumming fingers, wringing hands, tapping pens, breaking pencils, scratching, touching your clothes or jewelry, all add up to nervous, scared, lacking conviction, uncertain, and intimidated. Even if you do feel any of these, which we all do sometimes, don't show it—even a little. No one will ever say, "Joe, please stop wringing you hands." They will just be busy updating their résumés to get out of the organization that you run because of the lack of confidence you display.

I know of one CEO who gesticulates so frantically that he's been known to inflict cuts on his face. Talk about self-sabotage!

Other parts of the body assist the speaker but the hands speak themselves. By them we ask, promise, invoke, dismiss, threaten, entreat, deprecate. By them we express fear, joy, grief, our doubts, assent, or penitence; we show moderation or profusion, and mark number and time.
— Quintilian
Rhetorician, 1895

One of my favorite "hand" stories was from a CEO's spouse, "My husband and I have a reputation for holding hands at corporate and community events. Everyone thinks how charming and loving. Yes we feel that way. But it's also my way of helping him. Every time he starts talking too much I squeeze his hand. No one knows but him, but it reminds him to shut up and listen."

Smile

Whatever you do, don't forget to smile. You're the CEO! You have a lot to smile about. Besides, it's communicates your spirit—and everything we've been working on in this book.

Walk into a room, nonverbally tell people you're in charge (with your purposeful pacing and posture), and smile. Without the re-laxed, affable facial expression, you risk looking aloof, rude, sinis-ter, and cold. And worst of all, you look intellectually arrogant like "I don't need to deal with you."

Even when you have to face a difficult reality, you can still do it with a pleasant face. You can be tough and strong.

When Fidel Castro first visited the United States in 1959, his advisors told him to cut his hair and smile a lot.

Yes, it takes acting. Look how President Clinton kept at it all through the Monica Lewinsky scandal. You know that required *acting.* But what else could he do? Show what he felt and lose what followers he had. He had to try to still look like a leader. (Now I really shouldn't use him as an example at all. It's only that he is visible and we all know who he is and see him on the nightly news. I do believe he might have missed the first chapter in this book somewhere along the line—you know, be yourself, unless you're a jerk.)

A Japanese consultant, Yoshihiko Kadokawa, teaches Japanese to smile by having them put a chopstick between their teeth and than slowly pull it out. Voilá, a smile, "If you do not smile, you cannot make a profit," says Kadokawa.

Don't be fat

Thinness is a symbol of discipline, control, and perseverance. You don't need to be handsome or beautiful but you do have to have a "look" that is part military bearing and part corporate image. Plus an average weight:

- Keeps you healthier (a sound body reflects a sound mind, rightly or wrongly)
- Shows "self-command"

If you are going to carry excess weight, carry it well. Don't lumber and slouch. Maintain extra good posture and be "grand" in your appearance, not sheepish at all—like you're exactly the way you want to be.

A good friend of mine is a consultant and speaker. He told me about addressing 200 CEOs and said, "I was the only one ten pounds overweight." CEOs are *heavyweight*, not heavy!

Exceptional good looks are almost always a hindrance. People resent and don't trust someone who is too chiseled, manicured, and coifed. People respond to commanding behavior, not commanding looks. (And even that can be overdone. Anything good, taken to the extreme, becomes bad.) Look at the folksy Bill Gates or Warren Buffet. They don't look like yuppies. In fact today, you can get shot down before you get into the door if you aren't sufficiently geeklike.

Now you tell me, wouldn't it be nice to be described by others as "he walks into a room the way everyone in the world would want to…or gives a speech…handles the media…or deals with his board…or manages Wall Street the way everyone in the world would want to"?—well that takes theatrics. Rehearse over time when you aren't "on" the hot seat so when you're "on," it becomes second nature to you.

One of the CEOs I interviewed gave me his personal goal when working with people. To share it, I agreed not to name him, but I liked what he said and felt you would to. "I want to appear as a responsible human being. I want them to assume that I'm processing things quickly therefore I have to look and sit and talk like I am aware, alert, energetic. If I relax my bearing, my awareness of my physical impact too much it can reduce their confidence in me and I can't have that in my position.

I want to be prepared on whatever I'm supposed to do. I want them to feel that I studied it and that I'm on top of the details. I do that to show that I value their importance and position. I show them respect by my preparation and continuing effort while in that meeting. Regardless how powerful they are and intimidating they try to be, I let them know we are peers. There are no differences, we're all players, with no apologies. I respect them. I listen and respond. I will make good use of their time.

Again I have respect for them as well as myself. I know they are busy and I'm careful not to make them repeat themselves. I challenge them sometimes to keep them sharp but not to be offensive. And I wish to be gracious even in defeat because it's a temporary defeat. The next round I'll win. They just provided data so I'll win next time."

CHAPTER 8

EVANGELIZE
THE WORLD

♦ The CEO is the number one salesperson.
♦ How to get better at it.

Selling is one of the top three skills a CEO needs.
The other two are listening and delegating.

— Curt Carter
CEO, Gulbransen Inc. and America Inc.

An extra plus of being CEO is that your position gives you a chance to sell people others don't even get to meet, like other CEOs.

Sell is not one of those "bad" four-letter words. (Remember: you had to "sell" yourself to get to the position of CEO!)

"When I was in graduate school I imagined my first job would be in a high corner office where I could look down on things. I got offered a job in sales and I thought it was one level below child molester and one step above lawyer," says one CEO. "Boy was I wrong. I've since learned the CEO sponsored selling, integrity, and passion is the reason people buy."

The CEO *is* the top salesperson, company advocate, public relations spin doctor, evangelist, organization champion, cheerleader, and chief customer-relations officer—all of which takes selling.

A good salesperson has:

+ Personal and professional integrity

+ People skills

+ A goal, vision, or mission

+ Good cheer

+ A plan or an approach

+ Contacts, a network, and mentors

+ Effective communication skills

(Sound like what a worthwhile CEO has as traits too.)

"Those who can't sell can't be in business. Someone has to give you money, they don't do it willingly," says Jack Falvey, CEO of Intermark.

You're selling when you're speaking to the team, articulating your vision, implementing strategy, visiting the plant, recruiting talent, addressing the board, attending a business social function, talking to the media, guest lecturing at a university, dealing with a difficult vendor, schmoozing with investors, talking with analysts, *and* in conducting your communication in *everyday* business. You may not "sell" in the traditional sense of "closing the deal" but you influence, persuade, and get followership in the direction you want things to go. If you don't, who will?

Steve Aldrich, President of Quicken Insurance, says, "I sell all of the time. In every interaction I'm the ambassador for the company. I take pride in wearing shirts with Intuit's logo on it.

I was on an airplane and had our newest commercial on my computer. I kept playing it over and over hoping some people might hear it. I'm constantly trying to shape people's opinion of the company."

"Regardless of your rank you sell. The CEO is continually selling employees on staying with the company, selling the capital market to support the company, selling contractors to supply in the manner and timing you want, selling customers to buy," says Daryl Brewster, President of Planters Specialty Foods.

"Today the CEO is a foreign diplomat, statesman, and policymaker, too. CEOs meet with more heads of state in foreign countries than in our own," says Larry Dickenson, Senior Vice President of Boeing. That's selling.

You have to commit to selling and then do it, do it, do it, regardless of how uncomfortable you are.

All the power is in the hands of the customer.
— Gary Hoover
CEO, Hoovers.com

TO GET BETTER AT SELLING

Be ethical

I feel kind of silly saying this because it's so obvious. So I'll say, "speak straight" as a reminder.

If you're that "good" human being we've repeatedly discussed in this book, you create an environment of trust. Employees trust you and, in turn, customers trust employees. When the employees are "sold" on the company, they treat their customers better and customers buy more. When these things happen, investors get sold on the company too.

Know thy customer

The number one interest of people you are "selling to" is "what are you going to do for me?" That's a truism regardless of whom you are selling to: employees, customers, or anyone else.

"And that's true anywhere in the world," says Jim McBride, CEO of ATMO.

It's basic market research to find out what people want you to do for them. Learn their requirements. Find their pain. See how decisions will personally affect them. Understand their goals and their processes to getting there. Then, as possible, provide them with what they want.

Joe Galli is the new President of Amazon.com. He came from Black & Decker where he had the reputation of knowing more about his customers than they knew about themselves.

"Live in their world, not yours. Make it a way of life to listen to your customers. We blow up e-mails to poster size and place them on the walls around the company so everyone knows what the customers are saying....Every manager gets five customer names to call every day just to talk and see what they want," says Jeffrey Hoffman, CEO of Priceline Perfect YardSale. "To find out what customers want we just plain ask people. And when they buy we don't say 'thank you' we say 'congratulations.' That makes them feel better."

(*Important note*: A customer is a person who actually buys your product or service *and every other constituent* with whom you, as a CEO, deal!)

Be passionate

Or at least be whole-heartedly enthusiastic. Jack Daly calls himself Chief *Energizing* Officer of Platinum Capital Group. He also offers the four-word "shortest course in selling:"

"Ask questions and listen," says Daly.

(I'd offer another four-word approach: prepare, present, persist, perfect. Isn't that what this entire book is about really?)

Lawrence Land says, "When someone calls me I say, 'I'm so glad you called' not some version of 'yeah, wha da ya want.' It takes the wall down and sort of parts the red sea to get into the conversation."

Passion is contagious. So is a lack of it.

Be focused

If you don't know what you're "selling," what will people know to "buy"?

The story goes that when IBM was having a tough time several years ago, they were trying to be all things to all people. When asked, "What is your strategy?" by Steve Metzger, CEO of SPC, a senior IBM executive replied, "We are focused on vertical markets to bring targeted solutions to those customers."

"Which verticals?" asked Metzger.

"Why, all of them, of course."

Another story relates that when Morita Sony founded the Sony Company, he had his focus decided on before a single product was made. The saying was, "It's good, but it isn't a Sony." He decided what he and his company would stand for and he lived it.

Be focused on your next phone call, meeting, or event that you are attending. Focus on what you're going after. If you haven't got the time to think that through, how will you know what you're going after? Wait until something hits you on the side of the head?

Be available

Customers need to see you. Your salespeople need to see you and your constituents need to see you.

You have to meet customers. *They like* to meet you. That means you have to be out talking to people who buy what you sell.

It shows the CEO believes in the company product and supports its selling team. You're salespeople need to know that you know how difficult it is to do their job.

Before going in with a salesperson, ask the salesperson what he or she would like you to do. Don't go in like the "CEO stud," as one sales manager put it.

Help to deal with the hesitations and worries of the people to whom you're selling. Help others position your propositions realistically. Help to see possible compromises before going in.

Although Coach Vince Lombardi was talking about coaching, he was also talking about selling, "They call it coaching but it is teaching. You do not just tell them it is so, but you show them the reasons that it is so, and you repeat and repeat until they are convinced, until they know."

Salespeople can only truly benefit in the long run, when the salesman's being better off, follows the customer being better off.

— Stephen Metzger
CEO, SPC (Special Communities)

Check your effectiveness

If they say, "let me think about it," the answer is "no." Until you have a "yes," you don't have a "yes."

You have to pay attention to their reaction, to the message you're sending. You wouldn't necessarily ask, "How am I doing?" That's too personal. Instead, "What are we or aren't we doing well here?" and "What is our company good at, in your opinion or as it fits your needs?"

To ensure you're getting your message across, pay close attention to people's responses. Did they hear what you said in the way you meant it? Does it work for a positive solution for both them and you? Do they feel they are being heard? You may come in with you own ideas but when you listen to what others say, you have their ideas as well.

"When I lose a customer I'll call and ask why. It's hard to convince them I'm not trying to change their mind or get them to do business. Rather I just want their perfectly candid opinion. I ask, 'do me a favor, what didn't work for you. I want to get better.' When they say something I chime in with 'Good point.' Then I say, 'Thank you' and I send them a handwritten thank you note," says John Krebbs, CEO of Parker Album Company.

Studies show customers tell 18.5 people about their experience. The first exposure they have to you will get passed around. The new catchword is "viral" marketing—when word spreads about good or bad experiences.

Expect it to be difficult

If it wasn't everyone would be doing it.

Anytime you sell, there is rejection. Rejection is a good thing. From rejection you learn what to work on to get over it. Ashleigh Brilliant writes, "The difference between acceptance and rejection is that when you're accepted you don't have to try again."

Say you make some sales initiative five or six times a day. If you succeed one time, that's good. Most of what any of us do doesn't work *all* of the time. We all face adversity on an hour-by-hour basis. "Take your successes and blow them out of proportion and forget your failures," says Jack Falvey, CEO of Intermark. That's the beauty of the CEO job, say, as compared to the CFO. The finance person can't have just one out of six efforts successful!"

Smile when a "sale" is made.

In this chapter I've mainly talked about the CEO's role in "selling" his or her ideas, visions, strategy, etc. as opposed to hard-core, knock-on-the-door selling. The CEO *can* be the number one *cold-calling hard-core salesperson* in the company just because of his or her position. It's like Curt Carter's comment in the beginning of this chapter, "You can sell to people other's don't even get to meet." Carter talked about getting in the door to meet Ted Turner for a business deal and also former President Jimmy Carter. Carter is the only one in his company who could probably make that happen because he is the CEO.

Other CEOs recognize that power and use it. George Russell, Chairman of the Frank Russell Company, told me a story about the 1974 oil crisis when the price of oil shot up many times, resulting in lots of money going to Saudi Arabia. George thought the central bank might need his company's help (as the world's largest manager of money managers). So he made a *cold call* to the Saudi Arabian Monetary Agency Governor. He literally picked up the telephone and with no introduction he made a cold call. The rules then, and now, are that you must be invited to come to Saudi Arabia. (That fact alone would scare most people into inaction.) The Governor invited George.

Then George found a young Saudi at the University of Oregon to be his translator and together they traveled to have a meeting with the Saudi Arabian Monetary Agency. George was not hired. But as luck would have it, the young Saudi took George over to meet his uncle, who ran the National Commercial Bank, the largest bank in the kingdom. George did get hired there. "You never know what things are going to happen from a cold call," says George.

CHAPTER 9

GO BIG
OR GO HOME

♦ The CEO's role as a community leader.

It's not a significant part of the job. But, it is a significant part of who I am.
— Bernard Schwarts
CEO, Loral Space &
Communications

It is not your (official) job to be a community leader, doing charity work, and being an active social citizen. Your first obligation is to the company. That's what you get paid for. The CEO's job is to create value for owners. In fact, many say you shouldn't involve yourself with any activity that infringes on your time running the company.

Not surprisingly, there are lots of successful people who are not active "social citizens." "If I don't do anything immoral, illegal, or unethical, and I do put something back into my investors' pockets, I've fulfilled my responsibility," says one CEO.

Still others say the CEO job extends outside the walls of the corporate headquarters. You're now a public figure whether you intended to be or not. You can have a lot of "pull" in your geographic location and you have an obligation to give something back. There's a responsibility to get involved. You can't just be concerned about making money for yourself or your owners.

I don't seek personal press (that comes with charity events) and most CEOs I know don't either. I'm not comfortable with it. But someone advised me years ago that I have to understand how important it is to the company. It gives people pride in their company. It's part of being a leader. So I do it because of how it affects my people.
— Leo Kiely
CEO, Coors Brewing Company

In contrast to the individual who believes that staying a "good citizen" is sufficient, I heard from another CEO who literally takes on a new cause *every day*.

If you want to be involved, it's a personal preference and not professional obligation. "It's not the CEO's role, it's more of a personal thing. CEOs are too busy and it's difficult to be active and committed," says Hugh Sullivan, CPA. "If your customers are not in your local community but worldwide there's little direct benefit to the business. The benefit is for your self-esteem, personal growth, and satisfaction."

Although your customer base isn't in the community (say like a bank's would be), your employee base is. And being "involved in the community" can make your company a more visible and enticing place to work.

"Even if you don't sell directly to your community, your employees come from there. You need to make your company attractive to those living there. Plus you help the economy of the community which makes for a stronger community," says Bob DeWaay, Senior Vice President of Bankers Trust.

Steve Case of AOL believes companies need a strong commitment to the public good to attract the best people to work there *and it is those people who will, in turn,* generate that increased shareholder value.

The community created an opportunity for me and I feel a warm connection to it, so I give back.
— Bill Warren
CEO, National Inspection Services

It's possible to combine charitable work with a direct benefit to the organization. That's what the CEO of PepsiCo, Roger Enrico, does. He voluntarily reduced his salary to $1 and has asked that $1 million be contributed to a scholarship program for children of full-time employees who earn less than $60,000. (Now he still collects his bonus tied to the company's performance, which can be in the millions.) Enrico says, "In my opinion no one is more important than the thousands of men and women who make, move, and sell our products." He himself received a scholarship from his father's company when he was a boy, enabling him to get an education, and, as he sees it, eventually make it to CEO.

"I do fundraising for the Vietnamese-American community because the beneficiaries are mostly young people who are our future. I came from there, I know how hard it can be and how huge a difference it can make to have the opportunity for a decent education," says Quin Tran, Vice President and GM Worldwide of Xerox Colorgraphic. "Plus I do this because I want to give and make a difference for people who are less fortunate."

Your personal interests may determine the support. "Education and arts is a personal interest but supporting schools for development of students is different. With company money and company time there must be a payoff for the business in the long run," says Stuart Blinder, CFO of ITOCHU International.

So you give because you:

+ Feel lucky yourself.

+ Want to help others.

+ Can offer needed expertise.

+ Want to do more than just make money.

or even because you:

+ Want to keep in a high-profile arena.

+ Want to stay in front of prospective clients/customers.

+ Will benefit in giving public support.

+ Want to make good contacts.

But I don't believe donating to the Boys Scouts, United Way, Symphony Fund, or March of Dimes is the first kind of "giving" you should do. *Every good act is charity*: a smile, some praise, helping others feel they are contributing to the world, or allowing people to make mistakes and learn....The list is endless and it begins in your home office. Going outside to "give" for pride and ostentation, publicity and vanity, or any level of disguised ambition, is *not* charitable *really*.

BE ON BOARDS

The most prevalent activity for CEOs is being on boards—for the purpose of helping the organization succeed. The CEO uses skills honed for his or her for-profit company to benefit the nonprofit organization: vision, strategic planning, operations, getting and keeping good people, finance, leadership, and sales.

You must act in good faith, pay careful attention, and be diligent in your advice. "The board members listen and coach; provide focus and discipline; aid in staffing; debate strategy and direction; and guide financing," says Ken Olson a private "angel" investor for high-tech start-ups and expert on the role of corporate boards.

I've taken the traits he lays out as necessary for a corporate board and transferred them to the nonprofit board. Ken suggests these characteristics make up a good member so this is what you need to be offering the charitable (and corporate) boards:

+ Experience
+ Dedication and attentiveness
+ Ability to help the organization move up
+ Calmness and thoughtfulness
+ Open to new ideas
+ Ability to "tell it like it is"
+ Creativity
+ Willingness to grab a paddle and get wet
+ A good rolodex

"I decided never to be on a board unless I could be a good participant and I never wanted to get that emotionally involved," says one CEO. So don't. But if you do, do it well like you do everything else. That's 1000 percent. And that makes for good karma.

SET AN EXAMPLE

By being involved, you set the example for employees. Unless you send a strong message of expectation for community involvement, it typically doesn't happen by giving money, time, or expertise. You have to motivate others to get them involved.

And you need to make it easy for them to become a part of something. For example, Fannie Mae gives employees 10 hours of monthly paid volunteer time. McKinsey & Company loans out its employees for causes. American Express, Schwab, and many others do, too.

"Until you do get involved you can't imagine the value. Besides, if the CEO doesn't get involved why will his people know to do it? The community is who I sell to. I have a responsibility to get involved," says Steven Toups, CEO of Turner Professional Services. "That means me personally and when my people take an hour off to go to a planning meeting I don't get grumpy about it."

GIVE MONEY

You can give money. That's pretty straightforward. Altruism at any level is good.

Some CEOs say, "give money or time, but not both." "Not true," says Danita Johnson Hughes, CEO of Edgewater Systems for Balanced Living. "Give both when possible." (More is going to be expected from Microsoft than Ace Television Repair.)

If you combine the money with the intellectual capital a CEO has to offer an organization, then you truly add value.

"Some people indict the executive who only shows up with a check. The bigger the check the more disdain. I'd have to disagree. Corporate resources are severely constrained. When someone decides to earmark his/her precious budget dollars for a community project or non-profit organization, everyone should be thankful. Money shows commitment," says Mindy Credi, Director of Executive Learning, PepsiCo.

The truth is "charity" can be met with ingratitude—because no matter what you do or give, there will be critics who think you aren't doing enough. And you can, in fact, end up being of little service. *But* it can still make you feel good, like you're fulfilling a duty.

THE OTHER BENEFITS OF BEING A SOCIAL CITIZEN...

If you make your money from the local community, then supporting it is pretty important. You just might get the city council to vote for your plan to turn your vacant lot into a high-rise instead of keeping it in the low-rise zoning. Or you might get the legislators to back your development plans.

"No company exists in a vacuum. You need to communicate your accomplishments to the outside community to win support and understanding," says Peter Cimoroni, CEO of Millenium Grappler.

"At first, I thought I had to be involved in the community to build my business. Now I don't have to but I still want to help make a difference. I just choose my battles more." Says Jim Sherry, CEO of Sherry Consulting. "I always refer to a motto that is framed and hangs in my office, "Don't let things happen to you, *make* things happen."

GO BIG OR GO HOME

If you do decide to get involved in the community, *go big or go home*. The worst thing you can do is pledge to help and then renege. You fail if you "sign up" but don't deliver, where you get involved but don't ever do anything. You see it every day where companies pledge involvement for the prestige of the association or join boards for the contacts where there are other CEOs they want to be around.

And the sole purpose for getting involved shouldn't be for potential business. One CPA firm lent a hand with the total expectation of getting the organization's business. When they didn't, the CPA withdrew the support.

"The worst situation one can find is lack of financial commitment and a lack of engagement. To be affiliated with a cause to 'build one's résumé' is an unfortunate situation, but it happens," says Mindy Credi, Director of Executive Learning, PepsiCo.

You shouldn't do it because you:

♦ Get to meet important people and make good contacts.

♦ Will get your name printed in the paper or on some brochure.

♦ Look good to a group you want to influence.

♦ Think you know it all.

♦ Want to get more from the group than you give to the group.

"If people agree to serve on a board and get the recognition for it, my expectation is participation in some form. It's not fair to those that are out there procuring items, gaining corporate sponsorship, and attending meetings for someone's name to be included and recognized when they are not giving any effort. If you can't make the time, you shouldn't participate on the board. Plus if you commit to doing something and don't follow through it leaves a lack of credibility and trust with people," says Michelle Monfor Fitzhenry, Vice President of TRRG.

"Do it well or don't do it al all. There's no middle ground," says Lee Roberts, CEO of FileNET.

Commit and follow up. There is no judgment here as to whether you should or shouldn't get involved in community activities, but if you decide to get involved, come through with your commitments. That is the biggest complaint organizations have about a CEO in community activities. It's back to the integrity thing.

My involvement is about who else I can help to bring to success and happiness.
— Nimish Mehta
CEO, Impresse

CHAPTER 10

CUT THROUGH
THE JUNK

♦ How to achieve balance in your life for
  complete success.
♦ Do something toward it every day.

---

*I have 1000 things on my "to do" list and I'm on
number 8. And nine more just got added.*

> — Chris Vargas,
> CEO, F-Secure

A CEO has to do a *lot* of stuff, and a whole *lot more* if he or she wants to do it really well. At the end of the day (or rather the start of it), you need *to cut through the junk* that people want to put on top of you. You must set limits on other people taking your time and match what you're doing with what's important to you. You have to select, choose, and prioritize how you spend your time and then balance that with your responsibility as CEO.

It's difficult. I know. "Corporate Gods are not very forgiving and they ask you to make tough decisions," says Paul Schlossberg, CEO of D/FW Consulting.

"I just have to remember what's important and do it. That's my balance," says Quin Tran, Senior Vice President of Xerox Colorgraphic. As you work to do every other part of the CEO job 1000 percent better, work on doing the same for your own private life. You have to take care of yourself to be beneficial to others. If you don't strike some workable and satisfying balance between work *and* family, work *and* social, social *and* family, body *and* mind, and mind *and* soul, you won't be very happy and won't set a very good example— either for your employees or your children.

"Balance is an old phrase. It implies equality, which it never is. One spends more time at business than out of business but you still have to have a life," says Steward Blinder, CFO of ITOCHU.

A successful balance is a blur between work and play. "Balance is having a life outside of work that you enjoy as much as work, sometimes more," says Bruce Swinsky, President of Kodak Imaging. (*Note*: Balance is not to be confused with the new Las Vegas invention: a combination treadmill and slot machine.)

Everybody wants more balance. Jack Linkletter is a radio commentator on leadership. Like me, Jack talks with lots of CEOs. He asks them, "What is the most dramatic change you want to accomplish personally and professionally in the next three years? The number one answer is 'for personal and professional balance.'"

Balance is very important, particularly on the health side.
You need to consider it more than the balance sheet.

— Mark Pasquirella
Chairman, CEO, and President, Crown
American Realty Trust

Believe me, very few CEOs can honestly say, "I have it *totally* together and things are exactly how I want them to be." Some just have more workable solutions as a result of trade-offs that are acceptable to them and people close to them. It's like Oprah Winfrey says, "You can have it all, but you can't have it all at once." To take care of yourself while working hard, be:

+ Flexible

+ Tolerant of ambiguity

+ Able to keep things in perspective

So you strive for some semblance of balance anyway. Again, if not for yourself, for the people around you. Most CEOs "preach" it to some degree. They had better! You have to set the example. If you only show backbreaking hours to your people, they won't want to work for you. Unless you show that you "have a life" elsewhere, you don't really give people permission to do the same. In a tight labor market you have to openly display attempts in your own life to reinforce the possibility in their lives.

If you don't, you will end up with employees who work so hard they get numb and they won't be as sharp as they could be. Eventually, they will burn out, leaving a wake of wrecked marriages and troubled children, have midlife crises, and you end up with the expensive and time-consuming process of recruiting their replacements after they've left for Tahiti.

Employees demand more balance than ever in their work environments. If they see a CEO with a shower stall in his bathroom and a cot to sleep on in the boardroom, that is a bad sign.

In the world of sailing there is an expression, "one hand for the ship, one hand for you." It came from the old days and the big rigs where the sailors had to climb the masts to fix something. They had to do the work with one hand because the other hand was used to hang on. Fifty percent for you and 50 percent for the "ship" may not always work but it's something to strive for a little every day.

"My number one job is husband and father. My little girls are at the stage where Daddy is wonderful, and I love it. They want to marry Daddy! It scares me to death to think of them growing up and me missing it. I don't do anything but work and family. I don't hunt. I don't play golf. I don't want to be like my friend whose financial success cost him his daughter and wife," says Steven Toups, CEO of Turner Professional Services. "Balance is like a teeter totter. You just go back and forth. It reminds me of watching a car race on television where they put the camera inside the car. The driver always has his hands moving. Life is a series of right and left corrections because you want to keep it in the middle of the road and not hit the wall."

BALANCE IS A SIMPLE CONCEPT SO THE QUESTION IS WHY IS IT SO HARD TO DO?

Some say the CEO job is not a job for well-adjusted people.

For a lot of 40-plus–year-old CEOs success is bred by insecurity, trying to prove something to their fathers, fear of failure, or a reason to brag. Those "drives" aren't conducive to balance in life. One man who admitted being in that frame of mind "woke up" when his wife advised, "Make a lot of money, dear, so you can afford your next divorce."

People are afraid to pull back the reins because once you start winning, your bankroll changes as does your status in the community, and even your families perception of you. It's scary to do anything that would hinder any of that.

Some people prefer work life to home life. A CEO friend wrote me a note, "Debra, as you know I have been married and divorced four times and in each case the primary reason was my 100 percent devotion to business. And, all of my ex-wives were beautiful women! I've learned from watching others who successfully take care of their family and their work, but I'll still remain single."

More than one CEO has said to me that they love their work so much that if it came between choosing work or family, they'd take work.

Reminds me of the Katherine Hepburn quote, "If you always do what interests you, at least one person is happy."

"I do what I love so it's really not work. Far too many people never discover their craft. It exists for everyone. Most aren't willing to spend the time, effort, and pain. I was a high school teacher and wanted to make more money so I started working part-time at Arby's and loved it. I was still around kids, around food, around customers," says Russ Umphenour, CEO of RTM, who owns 120 Arby's. "I've kept an article for 15 years titled 'the myth of a balance.' If you really want to achieve something you need to be really committed and that creates imbalance. Now you can communicate to your family and friends better when you're going through those periods. And you do have to take time to get away from it all."

You can love what you do, but choose what you do, communicate your action, and don't try to do it all. Striving for balance *is some balance in itself.* Like everything in life, it will never be perfect. "It's just simple, *constant* effort. To create balance in my life, I try to exercise regularly. I'm a runner so I try to work out five to six times a week. Also, my husband and I go out to dinner and a movie almost every Friday without fail. This is our time together," says Dinita Johnson Hughes, CEO of Edgewater Systems for Balanced Living.

GET ON THE "SAME PAGE" WITH YOUR FAMILY

A "partner" who understands your obligations helps to make a relationship workable. So with two-way communication—and heartfelt sharing—explain your obligations and what it means. "Make certain what is important to you also meshes with what your family expects out of life," says Ron Brown, CEO of Maximation. "If the two do not balance, you will not be successful because no matter what, you will fail in one of the two areas."

"It's like you do in strategic planning but you do it for your family. I sit down and talk to my wife and discuss what's important to us and why it's important. Then we plan accordingly," says Steven Toups, CEO of Turner Professional Services.

You need a good soul mate to make the sweat and tears worth it.
— Dr. Kelvin Kesler
CEO, Ft. Collins Women's Clinic

"I could never have been as successful if I hadn't had a wife like mine who kept it all together at home. And over the years, I had to fire a lot of people who didn't have wives who were like that," says Ernie Howell, Retired President of WPM Packaging Systems. "We'd taken the kids to the mountains for a weekend and on the way home I told the kids about a job offer I was considering. I explained it meant a lot of travel, a lot of time away from home. My fourteen-year-old spoke up, 'It's okay to take the job, because the time you do spend you make meaningful.' And that's what you have to do. At work, you give it your all; when with the family, you give it your all."

Wynn Willard, President of Planters Ltd., has moved his family so frequently with job promotions that they have a standing joke, "we move before we get the bathrooms dirty." Willard continuously strives to keep his family involved. An example he gives is the time he brought the company's promotional vehicle home—a 24-foot-long Mr. Peanut hot rod—and took his sons for a ride around the neighborhood. Do you think he was a hero or not that day!

Every part of this book is to help you do your CEO job. Every part of the advice can be applied to your personal life as well. Just as he schedules his professional day, Barry Lathom, President of Xerox Colorgraphic, schedules his personal activities. "Family is very important to me. Without my wife and kids who knows where I'd be. If work impacts my family life, I change work. For example, I keep a calendar with everything I need to know about my family activities. It's very organized and I manage to it. When I schedule business appointments I do not conflict with the personal calendar. The worst thing to do is miss critical things in your family's life."

Treat people, especially your family, well. Give them the time they deserve.
— Bill Stavropoulos
CEO, The Dow Chemical Company

Another company president who schedules "family time" is Daryl Brewster of Planters Specialty Foods. "This afternoon my eighth-grade daughter was running for student council president for her school. So I took off at 1:15 for an hour and went to watch her give her speech. I plan time with kids, family and friends."

The same communication that is necessary up and down the ladder in the business is required in the home life. Desire and effort can make it happen. Now if the desire isn't there, the effort won't be. It's that simple. For example, according to *Men's Health* magazine, 9 percent of men polled would trade their wives or girlfriends to be a sports star. Hhmm.

There are ways you can do your job 1000 percent and still achieve personal and professional goals. Steve Aldrich told me he based his company in Alexandria, Virginia, because his wife had lived there. "I knew I'd be working 18 hours a day and traveling a lot. She'd be home alone but have her family and friends. And when we are together we focus completely on each other. We exercise together. Have dinner together. And I do day trips as much as possible instead of staying over night somewhere."

You probably can already guess that single (or soon to be single) CEOs have the least interest or concern about balance. Of course, some admit that's why they remain single. They would simply rather put all time and effort into their business instead of a personal life. At different times in life one feels differently about things. This chapter is for the people who have decided—whether single or not—to strive for more balance.

TO GET MORE BALANCE, DECIDE TO DO SOMETHING ABOUT IT EVERY DAY

People don't like to admit they have a lack of balance; it's like saying, "I haven't lived right." But the fact is most CEOs work at a potentially unsustainable level. For that extra 1000 percent, you have to economize yourself: push where you can and retreat when you sense there is nothing more you can do.

"Today we have too many masters: something, someone, or yourself. I think it is important that those masters are not short-changed and I feel guilty when I fall off—when kids, wife, friends, partner, community, and special company events—all get less of me than I would like. But I do keep trying," says Ted Wright, CEO of Ampersand.

The late great coach, Jim Valvano from North Carolina State said shortly before he died of cancer to "Do three things every day: Laugh for your heart. Think for your mind. And bring your emotions to tears for your soul."

Earlier in the book, I had the world's longest list of leadership traits. I hope to top that with the longest list of suggestions for you to do a little every day to get more balance in your life:

* *Do 1 hour less* at the office every Wednesday. You'll find your productivity doesn't drop in a corresponding manner.

* *Say "no"* to everything but priority. At some point, people will stop asking, knowing you'll say "no" (which can be good or bad of course).

* *Stop wanting* so much unnecessary material stuff. Return something to the store that you bought and don't need.

* Make your significant other *laugh more*.

* *Call home* from work or from the road.

* Take your old clothes to a local *charity*. One CEO I know has an exact and limited number of pants, shirts, suits, and shoes. Every time he buys a "new" anything, he gives an "old" away.

* Think of something you're *grateful* for and then write a note of thanks to the person responsible.

* Contact an old *mentor* and hash out a problem you're working on.

* Dine by candlelight and music tonight—*even if you're alone.*

* Spend 15 minutes *outside* today.

* "OK" the in-house childcare program.

* On your next plane trip, take your own *healthy lunch* on board.

* *Say something nice* to the person in the elevator with you.

* Go away for the weekend and don't take your briefcase.

* Eat with chopsticks to *slow down* your eating and let your food digest better.

* Have a barbecue where you invite your business colleagues and *their children*. Bob Galvin, Motorola's Chair, and his wife used to entertain this way so their children could get to know his people's children.

- *Write a letter* to your kids about what you're doing today and about some goal you're working on. Tell them what you hope for them as they go for their goals.

- *Write down your goals.* A Harvard study showed graduates who wrote goals down were three times more likely to achieve them than those who had the goals but didn't physically write them down. One CEO started a list in college of 100 things he wanted to do in his life before he died: drive a racecar, get a hole in one, have a poem published, etc. He's up to number 72 at last check. Write your own list.

- Write a letter to the editor of *Fortune* about an article you feel strongly about.

- Write an op-ed piece for *The Wall Street Journal*.

- *Take a writing class.*

- *Be a tourist for a day* on a business trip. Take a family member on the trip.

- Do some *vigorous exercise.* Your physical fitness is critical for your energy and good health. When you're young, you think you'll always have it, but that's the time you need to work on it *more* so you get into the habit and carry it on through life

- Sit up straight. Walk tall all day long, even on the way to the bathroom.

- Park your car a block away from every place you go. The publisher of *Glamour* magazine, Mary Berner, jogs home from the office every evening to save time going out and running, and she has her briefcase sent home by messenger.

- *Volunteer* yourself, your money, and your people at the town's next cleanup effort.

- Pick up the litter you see in your company parking lot.

- Listen to a new radio station. A study in Miami showed that after guinea pigs listened to music, they scored higher on tests of improved mood, less fatigue, less depression, and lower stress. (For extra enjoyment listen to some music you listened to in college.)

- *Listen* to a book on tape.

- *Listen* to a tape of your daughter's acceptance speech for class president.

- *Listen to the way you talk to others.* Take the edge out of your voice. (You can often replay the message you've left for someone on his or her voicemail to hear how you sound.)

- *Listen to the way you talk to yourself.* Cut out the negative self-talk.

- *Go home* and ride your Harley. "All you can think about then is staying alive," says Bruce Swinsky, President of Kodak Imaging. (Mike Moniz CEO, VR.1, can kayak or bike to work.)

- *Ask another company CEO* to give you a tour of his or her operations.

- *Ask a colleague* to join you on a walk as you thrash out an issue.

- If you catch yourself with a free 5 minutes, *enjoy it.* Don't fill it.

- Offer to *give a speech* at the local university.

- Do 100 more sit-ups today.

- *Learn* five yoga positions and do them. "Until I started doing yoga I took aspirin by the bottle in the middle of the night to deal with the tension," says one CEO in his 70s who has been doing yoga for 40 years.

+ *Smile* at six strangers today. (And 55 employees!)

+ *Climb the stairs* between floors. Keep your posture straight. Smile. George Russell is the chairman of the largest manager of money managers in the world. His organization controls trillions. Every day he exercises. Even if it means walking the fire stairs. When he travels, which he does a lot of, he makes time for exercise. Most frequently, it is going to the nearest fire exit and doing 30 minutes of aerobic walking up and down the fire stairs. "They are always available," he says.

+ Call a friend who makes you *laugh*.

+ *Send this list to a friend.*

People need to recreate to re-create. As the Speigel advertisement reads, "On the fast track, sometimes you have to pull over and park."

Even General Colin Powell says, "Take leave when you've earned it. Don't always run at breakneck speed."

If you don't, you risk becoming brain dead. "I was in Japan to give a speech. I was jetlagged. Five hundred cameras were going off in my face. I started looking at the crowd and I went brain dead." Says Mike Moniz, CEO of YR.1. He took a minisabbatical by stopping off in Oahu, Hawaii, on the way home. He rented a car, drove to the north side of the island, went to Ted's bakery, bought the "best macadamia nut" crème pie in the world, drove to the beach, and sat and ate the entire pie as the sun set.

If you are going to be a CEO, you are going to have to spend a disproportionate amount of time on business so you must make time and get value out of that time with coworkers and with the rest of the world.

DON'T REGRET THE PAST, CHANGE THE FUTURE

You've heard the expression, "No one has ever said on his or her death bed, 'I should have spent more time at work.'"

You have to desire balance to ever hope of getting any. I recall an e-mail I received from a friend, "As I have told you, C. and I are getting a divorce. Not wanting this and feeling I was not given the opportunity to correct what went wrong, I feel had I been more aware during the years we were married I might have been able to see the signs earlier that something was wrong. In hindsight, had I been able to pick up on those warning signals, I might have been able to take corrective action."

"If I had to do it all over again I'd spend more time with my family. I did have rules. Saturday and Sunday till 3:00 were off limits to work. Now I'm retiring and all I can say is, I wish I knew then what I do now about spending more time with my family," says one CEO.

"When my son Keeton moved in with me about 10 years ago I was running the company by myself and traveling a lot. It took 2 years, but I brought in extra people to help me and managed to cut my traveling by 60 percent. The first thing I do before starting a meeting is to be clear on the time we expect to finish it. If it goes on too long I request that we teleconference it. As a single father I often feel overcome with guilt because I have to leave work. But if I am not there, my child stays alone," says Peter Marcus, Chairman and President of QFTV, Inc.

From now on be adamant about setting time aside for family and fun. You look like a hypocrite if you promote flexibility but exhibit none. Plus you could cause bodily harm to yourself.

"My wife and daughter are always the most important people to me. And I will always give up sleep to work through the night so that I can spend a few hours with them in the evening. Even good CEOs must find time to play with Legos and Barbis!" says Douglas Neal, CEO, of Mobile Automation Inc.

Make time for yourself. "I take 1 day off every 2 weeks and every quarter, 1 full week off. It's inspired me to work harder so I can afford the day off. I have discovered balance this way. And I've found your income doesn't suffer. If you wait until you have the time, say when you're 70 years old, it's too late. You'll probably just end up dead," one CEO told me.

(Which might have been taken to the extreme when I recall talking with one e-commerce CEO who had taken three-3 month sabbaticals before he was 35 years old.)

Here is a present. It is one man's personal description of balance and it's a pretty picture for you to reflect on.

"Balance in Life? It's sorta like being in bed with a beautiful woman, great sex, discussing the upcoming elections, having a great Merlot with a delicious egg salad sandwich on Rainbow bread. That is balance.

Having a stack of books at your bedside. One on Ansel Adams' photo techniques, one by the Dali Lama on his latest reflections, one on the history of the Porsche auto from 1927 to 1983, and last but not least, Gary Larsen's latest cartoons.

Having a photo collection from places all around the world and a quiet garden to sit and enjoy them.

Skiing hard all day and surfing the net at night for the latest software systems.

Going to Israel to set up a new venture capital fund and being sure to spend a few days at Petra.

Going hunting with the guys from the body shop and avoiding discussions on capital markets. Taking your walkman with you and a good book on tape so that if an elk does cross your path you won't hear it and have no need to shoot it.

Oh yes, I forgot to mention that you should spend every Friday evening that you can with your mother and you should try to spend as many weekends as you can with your kids. This can be balanced with negotiating joint venture agreements for your overseas clients," says Norman Singer, CEO, of Israel Technology Partners.

Life is too short and there's too much fun to be had. "It isn't a good idea to defer joy for the long term. You have to squeeze a little joy in every day," says Jack Falvey, CEO of MakingTheNumbers.com. "You'll live longer and be happier."

WRAP-UP

♦ It's up to you, sorry to say.

_____

I'm still a "work in progress" and I expect to be for some time. But I'm having fun.
— Monique Robitaille
CEO, G. Brouilette & Son

Write your own ending. With some luck, with the things you learn along the way, and with some stuff you actually planned – it can be a great story!

"In this world, you're either on the stage, in the spotlight, or you're in the pits serving drinks," someone once said to me.

You're on the *edge* of winning *if* you'll do what I've laid out in the previous chapters.

How to *act like an effective CEO* is as difficult or as easy as you want to make it. There are really only two ways to fail:

♦ By trying and not succeeding

♦ By not trying at all

I've outlined the requirements to help you succeed. Now you have to use them regardless of whether your title is CEO. You need to use them even if your title is Dad, or Director, or Intern. The difference between good and great is that you've got to want it—to be that 1000 percent better. Some people just don't want it enough.

I know, it's still scary to try. There's nothing harder than being given your chance.

But now you have it. There's nothing to do but to do it. Life is all about turning things you want to do into things you've done.

And, remember, as I wrote in the Introduction, "if you don't get stronger and better every day, you get weaker and worse."

I sincerely hope you get everything you deserve and more. (I hope you don't experience being "passed early and often" as one person bemoaned to me.)

Remember, you are measured on *how* you accomplish things as well as *what* you accomplish.

FOR THE "GRAYS" OUT THERE...PLAYING THE *BACK NINE*, SO TO SPEAK (OR AS ONE PUNK PUT IT, "THE PEOPLE WHO PROVIDE ADULT SUPERVISION")

You are not finished at 40. And do not let an *NBC News* report affect you *more* then momentarily when they irresponsibly report that a person's productivity peaks at 43.3 years of age.

"I was the young person at the table for a long time. Now I'm one of the gray hairs. I was at a department store and someone was trying to locate me. When he did I asked how did he find me? He said he was told to look for a tall, gray-haired man," says one CEO who still races automobiles on the weekends. He added, "My generation used to not trust anyone over 40, now it's not trusting anyone under 30." (We're always startled when we're called "old" for the first time.)

Older people have as much of a career future as young people; it's just that the time to do it is compressed. Look at where you've been and honestly evaluate if you want to spend the rest of your working career doing the same thing. If not, now's definitely the time to change. That would be wise.

Woe to the person who has become old without becoming wise.

Old age starts the instant your attachment to the past inhibits your excitement for the future. "Even if you're on the right track, you'll get run over by the train if you just sit there," said the late Will Rogers. What can you do but keep trying something new? To compete with the younger ones, you have to *have* and *show* enthusiasm and energy. And, most importantly, you can't get trapped in "how much you know" because of your age. The more you think you know today, the less you learn tomorrow.

Just as at any point in your life, you need to be first, best, or different. First may not be the option now but the other two are.

Regardless of your history, you can make more history. Your experience becomes your memories and your memories become your history.

+ Don't object to new things too much.
+ Don't consult and analyze too long.
+ Don't act too conservatively.
+ Don't accept mediocrity in yourself.
+ Don't stop getting educated in the ways of the world.
+ Don't criticize young people for doing what you did when you were young yourself.
+ Do make friends with young, up-and-comers—they're going to live longer than friends your own age.

One CEO told me, "At 56 years old the downhill luge path is so fast it's unbelievable."

FOR THE PUNKS

First of all, they don't know your age, few will ask your age, and age won't be an issue, unless you make it one.

Also, don't ever feel you are in over your head (at least more than momentarily)—most everyone else is too, regardless of age or experience. That's what makes it so exciting.

The trend, particularly among the dot com company CEOs is to: (1) pull money together for funding, (2) try to manage to keep out the venture capital firms who provided that funding, and (3) work to sell the enterprise they created so they can start again. Don't remove yourself from the emerging CEO position altogether. Enjoy the challenge of wearing lots of hats and dealing with limited options. That's also where some fun comes in.

I want you to have the security of knowing that you have what it takes to be an exceptional leader. Whether you are one who has hit it rich so far or not, I want you to be reassured that you are on the right track to make it happen. Often, the unknown of what is required becomes intimidating. It's no longer unknown and it's not that complicated. But it does take effort and a little risk.

It's a great time to take risks when you're young. You can get by on—and away with—a lot due to youth. Today, more than ever, you have unbelievable opportunities to turn your idea into your livelihood. There is little penalty for failure. One CEO told me, "I should have gone early and often out of my comfort zone. You only have to be right one time. You can be wrong several times."

This is the time to:

♦ Build up habits, good habits.

♦ Pursue opportunities to really make something in this world and make a difference.

♦ Hope and dream.

♦ Use your God-given energy.

♦ Embrace your responsibility for the future world and the destiny of our nation and planet

♦ Go not for pleasure exclusively, but save some for later.

♦ Be most passionate.

Regardless of the money you make (whether it's a whole bunch or just enough), challenge yourself to develop into an exceptional personal "leader." Maybe you'll even want to be a professional leader but at least I hope you want to "stand out" for your own self.

You want to be a business version of a bachelor's description of the female he wants to meet, "a woman with a 50-year-old mind and an 18-year-old body."

Much of the great trends in our history came from youth:

♦ Alexander the Great conquered the civilized world by the age of 27.

♦ Alexander Graham Bell patented the first telephone at 29.

♦ Albert Einstein started his theory of space-time relativity at age 26.

♦ Samuel Colt patented the first revolver at 21.

♦ Ludwig van Beethoven published his *Opus I* by age 23.

♦ Petr Tchaikovsky completed his opera *Undine* at 29.

♦ And, of course, in modern times Steve Jobs and Bill Gates were 20 and 21 when they started their business.

It's tough to have wisdom in your 20s or even 30s, but that's what you need if you're in a position of power. At that age, you have lots of drive and energy to make your mark. You want to be a star. Yet, as a CEO, to be effective, you have to let others be a star. It takes wisdom and knowledge. It's a real struggle but it will give you many points on that 1000 percent improvement track.

As you get older, you'll need to rely on knowledge. While you're young is the time to develop skills in the CEO job. You'll get to "the top" faster, minimize mistakes, enjoy the trip better, leave fewer bodies strewn in your path, get into the two-comma crowd sooner, set an example for others, and build a legacy you can be proud of when you turn into one of the grays.

The downside of the early great success is that you probably haven't had enough experience in failure. Failure gives you the opportunity to grow and to become humble. "Without humbleness the decent person can become despicable and the despicable becomes unspeakable," says Peter Cimoroni, CEO of Millenium Grappler. Being young, successful, and a good human being is valued. Young, successful, and arrogant is tolerated *only* as long as you are needed.

"I feel sorry for people who didn't climb to the top but jumped there. They miss so much. They miss the challenge of it all. They jumped from kindergarten to graduate school. Often they didn't get the experience of acquiring communication skills, social decorum, diplomatic ability. Some day they will be middle-aged and old-aged and if they want to participate in the real world they'll need to know those skills," says John Bianchi, CEO of Frontier Gunleather.

That's one of the reasons for writing this book. To avoid that. If you experience early success, I want you to be able to repeat it. If success still eludes you, I want you to eventually enjoy it.

"I know I'm lucky. Can't quite figure out why but grateful nonetheless. Sometimes I sit back in the corporate jet and just chuckle inside wondering how I ever got here. Then when I pick up my car I go to the cheap gas station, just to keep things in perspective," says one CEO.

Regardless of your age, never forget where you came from; you might end up back there. Luck swings both ways. Sort of like the song, "with love, there are two ways to fall."

CEOs who act like I've described in this book get four to five calls a month from headhunters trying to recruit them into bigger jobs. But it's not easy. There's a lot of hard work involved. It's like the advice from country-western musician, Merle Haggard, speaking to someone getting into the entertainment business, "Get out. Or be prepared for a 35-year bus ride."

"The CEO job is never finished. You leave it so more people coming along can carry it on," says Jim Perrella, CEO of Ingersoll Rand.

I wish for you the words in the Frank Sinatra song, *My Way*, "Regrets, I've had a few, but too few to mention."

No matter how good or bad of a writer I am, if I've written a book that changes your life, I've achieved the only sort of success worth living.

So now, write your own ending.

SPECIAL THANKS

Nancy Albertini
CEO
Taylor-Winfield

Steven Aldrich
President
Quickeninsurance

Dan Amos
President/CEO
AFLAC, Inc.

Carol Ballock
Managing Director
Burson-Marsteller/Corporate
    Practice

John Biachi
President/CEO
Frontier Gunleather

Bud Bilanich
CEO
The Organizational
    Effectiveness Group

Stuart Blinder
CFO
ITOCHU International

Bill Blount
CEO
Power Motive Corporation

Christian Boucaud
Country Manager-Brazil
S.M.J. Beverages

Daryl Brewster
President
Planters Specialty Company

Ron Brown
CEO
Maximation

Robert Buhler
President
Open Pantry

Curt Carter
CEO
Gulbransen, Inc.

Helen Chacon
President
Common Ground Training

Linda Childears
President/CEO
Young Americans Bank

Peter Cimoroni
President
The Grappler Group

Kathern Cizynski
Senior Partner
Wiser Partners, Inc.

William Coleman
Chairman/CEO
BEA Systems, Inc.

Doug Conant
President
Nabisco Foods Company

Carolyn Creager
CEO
Executive Physical Therapy, Inc.

Mindy Credi
Director of Executive Learning
PepsiCo, Inc.

Jeff Cunningham
COB
iLIFE.com

Christopher Day
Co-president
Packtion Corporation

Jerome Davis
President
Maytag Commercial Products

Bob DeWaay
Exec. V. P.
Bankers Trust

Larry Dickenson
Sr. Vice President, Sales &
    Marketing
The Boeing Company

Jack Falvey
Founder
MakingTheNumber.com

Glen Fleischer
Vice President, Grocery
    products Unit
Nabisco Foods Company

Rev. Jim Forbes
Senior Minister
The Riverside Cathedral

Rich Gartrell
CFO
Goapply.com

Neil Georgi
CEO
Neil Georgi & Associates, Inc.

Sam Ginn
Chairman
Vodafone AirTouch

Frederick Glossen
CEO
MBI Industries

Joan Gustofaon
Vice President
3M

Jerry Henry
Chairman, President/CEO
John Manville Corporation

Gary Hoover
CEO
Hoovers.com

Dennis Hoppe
President
Hoppe Management
  Concepts, Inc.

Ernie Howell
Retired President
WPM Systems

Danita Johnson Hughes
CEO
Edgewater Systems for
  Balanced Living

Michael Jackson
Executive Director
Field Support
General Motors Corp.

Robert L. Johnson
Founder/CEO
B.E.T.

Sue Kanrich
Operations Training
F-O-R-T-U-N-E

Kelvin Kesler, M.D.
Chief of Staff
Fort Collins Women's Clinic

Leo Kiely
CEO
Coors Browing Company

Larry Kopp
Venture Capitalist

John Krebbs
CEO
Parker Album Company

Lawrence Land
Attorney at Law

Barry Lathan
President/CEO
Xerox ColografX System

Mary Lee
CPA

Stan Lewan
Market Manager, E-Commerce
IBM

Ed Liddy
Chairman, President/CEO
Allstate Insurance Co.

Jack Linkletter
CEO
Linkletter Enterprises

Gary Lyons
CEO
Neurocrine Biosciences

Peter Mackins
CPA
Visiting Nurse Association

Alex Mandl
CEO
Teligent

Dario Mariotti
General Manager
Mayfair Hotels

Peter Mannetti
President & CEO
US West Wireless, LLC

Peter Marcus
Chairman/President
QFTV, Inc.

Reuben Mark
Chairman, CEO, and President
Colgate-Palmolive Company

George Thome Matisz
President/Founder
Solotec Corp.

Nancy May
Founder, Managing Director
Women's Global Business
    Alliance

Jim McBride
CEO
ATMO, Inc.

Glen McCall
CEO
Global Venture Associates

Brian McCune
Managing Partner
e-merging technologies
    group, inc.

Nimish Mehta
CEO
Impresse Corporation

Steven Metzger
CEO
SPC

Mark Miller
Group Vice Pres.
Right Management
    Consultants

Steve Milovich
Chief People Officer
Walker Digit West

Mike Moniz
President/CEO
VR.1, Inc.

Douglas Neal
CEO
Mobile Automation

Christine Nazarenus
President
e-catalyst, Inc.

John F. O'Brien
President/CEO
Allmerica Financial

Rick O'Donnell
Director-Colorado
Office of Policy & Initiatives

Mark Pasquerilla
President
Crown American Realty Trust

Duane Pearsall
Former President/Founder
Columbine Venture Fund

Jim Perrella
Chairman
Ingersoll-Rand Co.

Dave Powelson
Chairman/CEO
TRI-R Systems

Lee Roberts
CEO
FileNet

Monique Robitaille
President
G. Brouillette & Son

George Russell
Chairman
Frank Russell Company

Paul Schlossberg
President
D/FW Consulting

Bernard Schwartz
Chairman/CEO
Loral Space &
    Communications, Ltd.

Joyce Scott
President
Strategy Consultants
    Consortium

Norman Singer
President
Israel Technology
    Partners

William Stavropoulos
President/CEO
The Dow Chemical
    Company

Hugh Sullivan
CPA

Bruce Swinsky
President
Kodak Imaging

Rudy Tauscher
General Manager
Trump International Hotel
    & Tower

Bill Toler
President
Campbell Sales Company

Steven Toups
President
Turner Professional Services

Quinn Tran
Vice President & G.M.
 Worldwide
Marketing & Sales
Xerox ColografX Systems

Michael Trufant
CEO
G & M Marine, Inc.

Russ Umphenour
CEO
RTM, Inc.

Chris Vargas
President
F-Secure, Inc.

William Warren
President
National Inspection Services

Craig Watson
Vice President/CIO
FMC Corporation

Mike Wilfley
President
A.R. Wilfley & Sons, Inc.

Wynn Willard
President & CEO
Nabisco Ltd.

Brad Williams
President
Dakota Beverage

Maury Willman
President/CEO
Willman Productions, LLC

W. Ted Wright, IV
CEO
Ampersand

INDEX

ABOUT THE AUTHOR

D. A. Benton founded Benton Management Resources in 1976 to provide executive development and career counseling. She has worked in 17 countries and her numerous media appearances around the world have brought her wide acclaim. Her clients include AT&T, American Express, Pepsi, United Airlines, Nabisco, Mobil Oil, PricewaterhouseCoopers, and NASA. Benton is also *The New York Times* business bestselling author of *How to Think Like a CEO.*